DIY HYDROPONIC GARDEN

The Complete Guide to Building Your Own Hydroponic System at Home for Growing Plants in Water

Walter Brown

By reading this document, the reader agrees that under no circumstances is the author responsible for any losses, direct or indirect, which are incurred as a result of the use of information contained within this document, including, but not limited to, — errors, omissions, or inaccuracies.

Table of Contents

INTRODUCTION

The technique of putting plants into a container with a growing medium and feeding it water with essential elements is the gist of hydroponic gardening. Almost all flowering plants, house plants, fruit plants, and vegetables can be grown using hydroponic gardening. It is an ideal way to provide your family and yourself with fresh garden products at any time of the year. Vegetables and fruits that grow on plants, as well as flowers, herbs, crops, and ornamental plants, are made available all year round through hydroponics.

Growing Medium is Needed

Without the use of soil, an alternative medium is needed to grow plants to provide nutrients and other essential elements.

Therefore, a growing medium is crucial to support the plants. One growing medium is polyfoam insulation – this growing medium is a more obscure one because it is not typically used in hydroponic gardening. However, because it is widely sold and cheap, many gardeners tend to use it as a starting medium as an alternate material to mineral wool or Rockwool and oasis cubes.

Types of Growing Media Used in Hydroponics

At the core of hydroponics gardening is the premise of growing your plants without soil or dirt. But you should keep in mind that whatever type of growing medium you might use, it cannot produce anything by itself. You still have to use it along with the nutrient solution to improve your herbs and vegetables hydroponically.

The various types of hydroponics growing media are as follows:

1. Rockwool

The resulting material, Rockwool, is cut up to form slabs, sheets, or cubes. Rockwool has the fantastic ability to quickly absorb nutrient solution (water), which is why you need to be careful about getting it too saturated to the point that your plants' roots become suffocated. Otherwise, you risk getting root and stem rot. Composed of granite and limestone, Rockwool is one of the most common mediums for growing hydroponic plants. It can often be bought in the form of sheets, blocks, cubes, and slabs. Granite and limestone are melted and spun into outstanding threads, which resembles cotton candy. Because of this, it can absorb fair amounts of water. However, the pH level and balance of a piece of Rockwool should be checked before use. You can try soaking Rockwool in water that has been pH-adjusted before using it as your hydroponics system' growing medium.

2. Coco coir

One of the best-growing mediums, coco fiber and chips allows sufficient space for the roots and the plant itself to breathe. It also excellently holds moisture and has a neutral level of ph.

Coco coir is organic. But since its decomposition rate is extremely slow, it can break down without having any of its components affecting the chemical composition of your system's nutrient solution. This means that coco coir does not get in the way of your plants being able to grow properly, which is why it is just right for use in hydroponics gardening.

Using coco coir as your hydroponic system's growing medium has a number of advantages. It naturally has a neutral pH, can retain moisture well, and provides proper aeration to your plants' root systems.

You can use coco coir to grow your herbs and vegetables hydroponically in the form of coco chips, which appear like small wood chips but are made of the same coconut husks that coco coir or fiber is made of.

You might consider using coco chips over coco fiber as your plant growing medium since the larger air pockets they provide allow your herbs and vegetable roots to be properly aerated.

3. Water-absorbing polymer crystals

Many industries have a use for water-absorbing polymer crystals – this type of hydroponics growing medium is actually used in making baby diapers, cooling sport cloths for the head and neck, and even soil gardening. Water-absorbing polymer crystals are also used in keeping cut flowers fresh for longer. Many people also find the colored ones pretty enough to serve as an inexpensive way of livening up the look of the inside of their bathrooms.

As the water-absorbing polymer crystals soak up the nutrient solution, they expand to several times their original size. In fact, as much as fifty gallons of water can be absorbed by just one pound of these crystals.

Water-absorbing polymer crystals can be purchased in different sizes. You can choose among those that are of the same size as golf balls and marbles, as well as those that come in powdered form.

4. River rock

River rock is a type of growing medium that consists of round-shaped and smooth-edged rocks which formed by being tumbled down the river. In the case of manufactured river rock, its similar shape and texture as that of natural river rock is a result of letting it run through huge mechanical tumblers.

You can purchase river rock in a wide variety of sizes. They don't cost that much, and you can easily find them in many home improvement centers as well as pet supplies stores.

If you would instead go for a rustic design in your hydroponics garden, then there is no reason why you can't use the regular jagged rocks lying around in your backyard. You only have to make sure that you have cleaned as well as sanitized them before you use them as a growing medium for your herbs and vegetables.

To clean the rocks, use your garden hose's jet spray to squirt off all the dirt adhering to them. Follow up with a thorough soak (overnight) in a solution of water and bleach to sanitize. After rinsing the rocks well with clean water, you may then use them in your hydroponics system.

5. Gravel

One of the most commonly used and easy to find substrates is gravel. Gravel can frequently be found in the ebb and flow system because of its weight and durability. That benefit, however, is also

10

what makes it problematic. Gravel can be challenging to carry around because it's heavy and can damage plants if you're not careful.

Another pitfall is that gravel is not porous at all and retains no water. You can't count on it if you have a power outage, so be sure if you do choose gravel that you watch the water nutrient levels and be sure that your plants are not drying out.

6. Perlite

Perlite is a type of growing medium that is made up of minerals that have undergone extremely high temperatures to make it expand. The heating process turns perlite into an extremely light material that is porous as well as absorbent.

Perlite is commonly sold in nurseries as it is also used in potting soils. But you might try purchasing it at stores that sell concrete mixes, mixing supplies, and other building supplies; sometimes, perlite is also a cement additive.

Before using it, you have to make sure that all of its dust particles are washed out and that it is wet. This will help in keeping the dust from being carried by the wind.

7. Vermiculite

Similar to perlite, the silicate mineral vermiculite also expands when it is subjected to extremely high heat. As vermiculite is extremely light, you might want to avoid using it in an ebb-flow hydroponics system, where it will tend to float.

There are many types of vermiculite, all of which have different uses, so you need to make sure that what you are buying from a nursery is the type intended for use in hydroponics gardening.

8. Sand

A commonly used growing media in growing hydroponic herbs and vegetables, sand, is similar to a rock. But since it is considerably smaller than regular stones, it does a better job at retaining moisture.

Its ability to keep moisture from getting drained out quickly makes it a good growing medium to use in combination with coco coir, perlite, and vermiculite.

If using sand as your hydroponic growing medium, you must use the biggest grain size possible. Doing so helps ensure that your plant roots will receive proper aeration, as a result of the increased size of the pockets of air trapped between the sand grains.

Pine bark (composted and aged)

This type of growing medium is among those first used in hydroponics gardening. Pine bark used to be thought of as a waste product; later on, it has been found to be useful in mulching garden soil as well as in serving as an active substrate for some hydroponically-grown fruits, vegetables, and herbs.

Many hydroponic gardeners find aged pine bark (to which less nitrogen has been added) a better choice over fresh pine bark, although using it as a growing medium can be more challenging compared to using composted pine bark. You can easily purchase pine bark at stores that carry ground mulch.

9. Rice hulls

Rice hulls are byproducts of rice production. They are commonly classified as aged, fresh, parboiled, composted, or carbonized. Although rice hulls are organic in nature, they have their use in hydroponic gardening as a type of growing medium since they tend to decompose at a very slow rate (similar to that of coco coir). Many growing media mixes sold in stores combine rice hulls with pine bark. You might consider avoiding the use of fresh rice hulls as growing media in your hydroponics garden. There is always the possibility that the fresh rice hulls you purchase could contain fungal spores, decaying bugs, bacteria, weed seeds, rice grains, and other contaminants. Composted rice hulls (and fresh rice hulls as well) usually contain high amounts of manganese. You can get around any issues with manganese toxicity by making sure that you are buying composted or fresh rice hulls with a pH level of more than 5.

10. Grow rock (hydro corn)

Grow rock is a form of clay. This clay aggregate has undergone a super-firing process that leaves it porous, lightweight, and expanded.What is great about using grow rock as hydroponics growing medium is that, although it is considerably light, it is still heavy enough to avoid floating in your system. Aside from providing adequate support to your hydroponic herbs and vegetables, grow rocks can hold moisture as well as wick up water (nutrient solution) to the roots of your plants. You can use grow rock as a hydroponic growing medium repeatedly, just make sure that it has been cleaned and sterilized before using it again. As grow rocks are quite popular among hydroponics gardeners, you can easily purchase them at almost all stores that sell hydroponic supplies.

11. Grow stone hydroponic substrate

While grow rocks are made of clay and are shaped like marbles, grow stone hydroponic substrate is made from glass that has undergone the recycling process and is unevenly shaped.Growstones are remarkable in their ability to effectively wick up nutrient solution up to a height of four inches above your hydroponic system's water line. This great wicking ability of grow stones can be its downside though, as it might wick water up to the top of your hydroponics system. The grow stones could end up being continuously wet and contribute to stem rot. This is the reason your grow stones must be deep enough and have good drainage. They are made of recycled glass, but their uneven edges are not sharp at all.

12. Oasis cubes

Oasis cubes share the same cube shapes and absorbent properties with Rockwool cubes, although oasis cubes work more like floral foams, which are usually used by florists to display their stemmed flowers. Due to their open-cell structure, oasis cubes can effectively absorb water as well as air. Moisture is wicked by the open cells throughout this growing medium, making it easy for your plants' roots to grow and expand. You can either use oasis cubes as starter cubes to grow your hydroponic herbs and vegetables in or use the bags (into which you place your plants' containers) they usually come with. What makes oasis cubes better than Rockwool as a growing medium is its ability to avoid becoming waterlogged, which Rockwool is prone to do. But it still helps to keep the oasis cubes from continually coming into contact with the nutrient solution to avoid any problems with getting them waterlogged. Oasis cubes are an open-celled material that enables the roots of the plants to expand all throughout the surface. It can accommodate the roots well because of the grid structure it has.

13. Coconut fiber

This is an organic material that is great for this kind of growing. It can hold air and water perfectly and has the bonus of being able to protect the plants from fungus. There are several different names that this comes under so you should look around for it. You will find it as a compressed block that will expand as soon as you place it into some water.

You Need to Choose a Growing System

Hydroponic gardening has two varieties: active and passive hydroponics. The main difference between the two is how hydroponic fertilizers are fed into the containers of plants, for the roots to absorb. Active hydroponics requires the participation of outside energy to pump water and nutrient solution to the roots, following a schedule. On the other hand, passive hydroponics does not require a schedule, but the mixture is constantly fed into the roots through capillary action. Another way to categorize hydroponic growing systems is through its ability to re-use unabsorbed fertilizers. Recovery systems can recirculate fertilizer that isn't used by the plants. They collect these and feed it again to the containers. Non-recovery systems are those that do not allow this reusing process. This includes humidity, lights, and pests. It is possible to enclose a hydroponic garden in a controlled environment to ensure that the plants will thrive, even if it is out of season. This can be done by the use of air humidifiers (for humidity) and grow lights for the illumination needs of your plants.

CHAPTER 1

UNDERSTANDING HYDROPONICS SYSTEM

Your hydroponic garden can be had without having to spend a lot constructing it. Instead of those packed with chemicals and pesticides, almost everyone wants to cultivate plants or own a garden to enjoy fresh produce. But with time, finding the proper size of the land for gardening purposes is getting complicated. But a modern-day alternative known as hydroponics has been developed to solve the problem.

In this chapter, learn how to grow organic plants in water with a hydroponic gardening system without wasting too much money or time all year round in your home or backyard garden.

History of Hydroponics

Hydroponics is an advanced technology that has its origins in the history of Earth. In reality, with ocean-going photosynthetic algae and photosynthetic bacteria, the oldest method of growth. That still happens in front of terrestrial plants and helps create the oxygenated air we breathe today.

One from the wonders of the Ancient World, in Babylon (hanging garden) , is the first recorded instance of hydroponics based on water. The gardens fllourish an intricate irrigation network that provided a steady stream of oxygen rich water and also minerals.

From the results of experiments performed to determine plant composition dating back to the early 1600s, modern hydroponics was developed, but plants were grown much earlier in soilless culture than this, even though it was not known as hydroponic. The world's rice crops have been developed hydroponically since time immemorial, as they are to this day.

The Central American Aztecs have developed an innovative method of using principles of hydroponics. Treated with animosity by their more influential neighbors and refusing any arable land, they discern how to build rafts of chinampas called rushes and reeds.

Chinampas were strong roots that were filled with sediment and lashed from the bottom of lake. Since the water came from the lake's bottom, it was rich in several organic minerals and compounds that the Aztecs used to grow plants and feed on.

The chinampas were often joined to form floating islands, for as long as two hundred feet guarded by rivers and canals of drainage. A certain chinampas had a place of residence for gardner. On days of market, the gardener would pole his raft near a marketplace, picking and delivering vegetables or flowers as they were bought by shoppers.

The chinampas supported abundant vegetable crops, flowers, and trees. The plant roots broadened through the chinampas floor, allowing a constant source of surface water and oxygenation.

When the Spaniards landed inside the New World, the look of these islands had already shocked Cortes. Historian William Prescott documented the invading Spaniards ' devastation of the Aztec empire, described the chinampas as "Wondering Islands of Verdure, overflowing with vegetables and flowers floating like rafts across the water."

The earliest known scientific approach to exploring plant growth requirements was in 1600, when the Belgian Jan Van Helmont demonstrated that plants are receiving water substances in his classic experiment.

He sowed a 5-lbs willow shoot in a tube consisting 200 lbs of insulated, dried soil to ensure precision. After five years of daily irrigation with rainwater, he found the growth of willow shoot by 160 lbs, whereas the soil lost less than 2 ounces.

His conclusion was correct that plants are for production receiving substances from water. However, he didn't know they also need airborne carbon dioxide and oxygen.

Modern chemistry theory made strides during the 18th and 17th centuries, and together with the scientific method, it revolutionized the nature of scientific study. The researcher's ability to work off a widely accepted base of chemical compounds enabled a more lively and presumptuous discussion of the essential nutrients needed to grow plants and laid the foundation for a modern understanding of plant growth requirements.

The English scientist Joseph Priestly discovered in 1792 that plants would slowly absorb it and give off oxygen when placed in a chamber with a high carbon dioxide level.

Few years later, Jean Ingen-Housz took a step further with Priestly's work and showed that plants in a carbon dioxide-filled chamber could replace the gas with oxygen in a few hours if the chamber was put into sunlight.

Ingen-Housz has continued to demonstrate that in bright light conditions, this process worked better, which involves the green parts of plants.

Through numerous experiments, scientists established plant composition during the mid-19th century, and the required substances to grow. It turned out that the soil itself has not been found to be of benefit to the plant for anything except supporting and sustaining the necessary mineral elements for production.

The complex role of humus and bacteria in healthy soil systems is, of course, a gross generalization. Nevertheless, it makes the way for a deeper understanding of basic plant needs.

Other than the soil itself, it turned out to be the minerals present in the soil, and the corresponding gaps (for oxygen) between them that the plants thrived. The next step towards the expression of the hydroponic technology was to remove growing media and produce plants growth in a salt solution that contained all the minerals needed.

Julius von Sachs, a botany professor in 1860 at the University of Wurzburg, published the first simple way for a solution of nutrients that could be dissolved in water and successfully grown in plants. The method has been called "nutritional." The precise number of plants that require elements is a matter of some debate. Some say 15, others 17. Nevertheless, as we can see, someone who appears to have a clear understanding of the basic requirements for working natural systems at full efficiency limits the natural order.

Plants want a lot more way than they need. And conventional methods for the hydroponic nutrients leave plenty to be desired. Nevertheless, it should be noted that hydroponic agriculture usually yields higher crops that is relative to the cost fertilizers used in standard agriculture.

Work on the practical application of nutriculture did not emerge until around 1925 when the greenhouse sector expressed interest in its use. There was a regular need to replace greenhouse soils to fix soil structure, fertility, and pest problems. Within a world of soullessness, all these issues were alleviated.

Even the groundless claims have done more to weaken hydroponic acceptance than they have done to help. Individuals feed on the hype generated by the press, focusing on selling worthless equipment to unknown customers trying to leverage the new "colossal breakthrough." The disdain offered by this farce lasted many years and left hydroponics technology dormant until it was unavoidable for our global endeavors.

There was a resurgence of scientific interest in hydroponics, and experiments with government funding started when World War II ended in 1939. The hydroponic units formed at military bases on several Pacific islands by the United States and British Army to supply the troops with fresh produce during the wartime.

During World War II, the military continued to make use of hydroponics as their only way of producing food abroad. The United

States Army hydroponic division produced more than 8,000,000 lbs of fresh in 1952, a record year for military production.

In the middle of 20th century, many challenges were overcome, including lax environmental controls, dishonest rising media, and the use of unsafe materials. Concrete used to grow beds was toxic and easily corroded iron pipes, which often leaked dangerous chemicals or radioactive material into nutrient solutions.

Hydroponics had arrived as a viable cultivation method, with the adoption of plastics by the mainstream in the 1970s. Plastics rescued the farmers from the costly building and destroying the properties of the device's first components. With the manufacture of suitable pumps, plastic plumbing and timers, it is now possible to automate, computerize, and streamline-media hydroponic systems to minimize both capital and operating costs. Hydroponics will now be available cost-effectively for both personal and business uses.

Hydroponics was used in the mainstream, and controversially it was adopted by the USDA for use in "organic" agriculture. Hydroponics now reflects the future. The technology solves food and water shortages, arguably the two big challenges of the 21st century. It can yield 10x per acre, and use only 1/20th.

Hydroponics has its drawbacks. That is to say, hydro usually provide what the plants want, not what they want. No system of growth will ever replace the system of crops grown underneath the sun. And it is with the goal that we should learn how to use this revolutionary technology to benefit humanity.

What is Hydroponics?

Look no soil! No water! We are so used to growing plants in fields and gardens that we consider something else wholly remarkable. Still, that's true. Plants not only thrive without soil but also thrive much better with their roots in water or very moist air instead. Soilless plants are known as hydroponics. It may sound odd, but many of the foods we eat, including tomatoes on the vine, have grown hydroponically already. Let's look at hydroponics a little more!

Plants grew through a process called photosynthesis in which they convert carbon dioxide (a gas in the air) and water into glucose (a type of sugar) and oxygen using sunlight and a chemical within their leaves called chlorophyll. Chemically, and you get this equation:

$6CO_2 + 6H_2O - C_6H_{12}O_6 + 6O_2$

There's no mention of "soil" anywhere in it, and that's all the evidence that you need plants to grow without it. All they need is water and nutrients, all of which are easily obtained from the soil. But if they can get those things elsewhere, say, by standing in a nutrient-rich solution with their roots, they can do without soil altogether. This is the underlying concept behind hydroponics. The term "hydroponics" in principle means plants are growing in water (from two Greek words meaning "water" and "toil"). Still, because you can grow plants without simply standing them in water, most people interpret the word to mean plants growing without using soil.

So why it is that things grow hydroponically?

While often the benefits of hydroponics have been challenged, there are a lot of advantages to growing without soil. Several hydroponic growers have found that when they turn from conventional methods, they get yields several times greater. Since hydroponically grown plants directly dip their roots into nutrient-rich solutions, they get much easier what they need than soil-growing plants. So they need smaller root systems and can channel more energy into leaf and stem growth. You can grow plants in the same area with smaller roots and get more yield from the same amount of land (which is especially good news if you thrive in a restricted area like a greenhouse or on a balcony or indoor window knowledge). Hydroponic plants are growing more rapidly, too. Most pests are brought in the soil, and usually doing without it would give you a more hygienic growing method with fewer disease problems. Because hydroponics is suitable for indoor cultivation, it can be used to grow plants throughout the year. Automated timer-and computer-controlled systems are making the whole thing a breeze.

This isn't just good news; there are always a few drawbacks. Another is the cost of all the required equipment containers, pumps, lamps, nutrients, etc. The panic aspect of hydroponics is another drawback: there's a certain amount of toil involved. For traditional growing, you can also be very cavalier about how you handle plants, and your plants will always flourish if the environment and other conditions are on your side. Yet hydroponics is more practical, and the plants under your power are even more so. You have to continually test them to make sure they develop in precisely the conditions they

24

need (though automated systems like lighting timers make it a little easier). The downside (probably less of a drawback) is that since hydroponic plants have much smaller root systems, they are not always able to be very well supported. Heavy fruiting plants would need pretty elaborate support sources.

How Does The Hydroponics System Work?

There are different ways to make things grow hydroponically. You stand your plants in a plastic trough in one \common process, and let a nutrient solution trickle past their roots (with the assistance of gravity and a pump). That's called the nutrient-film technique: the nutrient is like a liquid conveyor belt. It's continuously slipping past the roots, supplying them with the goods they need. Alternatively, a nutrient-enriched medium such as rock wool, sand, or vermiculite, which serves as a sterile replacement for soil, protects plants with their roots. Another approach is called aeroponics, and a standard product called the Aero Garden is typified for this. Effectively the roots expand a bit like a cloud packed full of minerals in a nutrient-rich aerosol.

By principle, you can grow any plant hydroponically, but some plants naturally do better than others—as is often the case with gardening. Among the plants that do exceptionally well are fruit crops such as tomatoes and strawberries and lettuces and herbs.

Importance of Hydroponics system

Hydroponics is essential because of its ability to dramatically alter the conditions a plant grows in.

This puts us in a situation to supply the plant with its unique needs (amount of nutrients, etc.) while still saving tons of water compared to traditional farming. This means a much more productive plant growing period, allowing for more harvesting.

Fortunately, more and more people are starting to see the potential in hydroponics, and someday, instead of our old systems, we might depend on this.

The plant's speed of growth is the crucial significance for hydroponics over soil growth. When you are growing something in the soil, watering your crop, you must feed the soil, not the seed. Then the soil retains the nutrients and makes them available to the plant. This phase is slower; that's not instantaneous. And if you have nutrient issues, you're not going to see the symptoms until the plant gets into the issue for a week. You then fix the issue, and you really should know the difference in the plant within about a week.

It is not like that in hydroponics; your plant is fed directly into the water through the nutrients. This has direct access to all of the nutrients. You will see the difference in two or three days instead of a week if you have issues, and fix it. Your plant will grow faster and grow larger. It's like buffet dining.

There are also other significant considerations, but in our opinion. This is the main factor making hydroponics more attractive than traditional agricultural soil. Hydroponics is like steroids, immediate exposure to all of the plant's nutrients required to survive.

Hydroponics can be used as a commercial vegetable production method, including tomatoes, seedless cucumber, lettuce, etc. Experiments on culture can be used to recognize critical elements and their role in plant structure and function. This can also assist in identifying the signs of an essential element's deficiency. It is achieved by performing a series of experiments in which plant roots are submerged in a solution of nutrients. Which an ingredient is added/removed or given in varying concentrations. In this way, we can find the optimum level needed by the plant for the proper growth of many minerals. Hydroponics is also useful in areas with thin infertile, dry soil. It can optimally control the pH for a specific crop. This also controls bacteria trapped in the ground.

Why to choose hydroponics?

Why go through all the trouble of hydroponic device setup? After all, people used good old-fashioned soil to cultivate food just fine for thousands of years, if not millions of years. Hydroponics provides some significant advantages over conventional farming, and as word spreads about these advantages. Many people turn to hydroponics for their agricultural needs.

First of all, hydroponics allows people to grow food, where conventional farming is simply not feasible. For decades hydroponics has been in use in areas with arid climates, such as Arizona and Israel. This science helps those living in these areas to enjoy developed locally and to increase their food production. Hydroponics is equally effective in dense urban areas, where land is at a premium. In Tokyo, hydroponics is used in place of conventional plant growth dependent on soil. For remote areas, such as Bermuda, hydroponics is also useful. With so little room available for planting, Bermudians have switched to hydroponic systems that typically take up around 20 percent of the land required for crop production. This helps the island's people to enjoy local produce year-round without the cost and delay of imports. Finally, hydroponics may help areas that don't receive sufficient sunshine or warm weather. Locations such as Alaska and Russia, where growing seasons are shorter, use hydroponic greenhouses to regulate light and temperature to achieve higher crop yields.

We do need to consider the significant environmental advantages of using hydroponics. Hydroponic systems need just around 10 percent of the water required by soil-based farming. That is because hydroponic systems allow water and nutrient solutions to be recycled and reused and because no water is wasted. It can have a significant effect on areas where water is scarce, for example, in the Middle East and parts of Africa. Likewise, hydroponics requires little to no pesticides, and just about 25 percent of the soil-based plants ' nutrients and fertilizers needed. This not only reflects cost savings but also protects the atmosphere by not introducing any contaminants into the air. Eventually, we have to consider the impacts of transport on the environment. Given that hydroponics allows production to be grown locally and requires fewer areas to import their crops, both price and greenhouse gas emissions are reduced due to reduced transport requirements.

First, hydroponics gives us a shorter harvest time profit. Plants grown in this way have easy access to water and nutrients, so they are not required to establish extensive root systems to find the nutrients they need. As conventional agriculture, this saves time and yields better, lusher plants in around half of the time.

Then why not hand over hydroponics? It is due to the distinct inconveniences associated with these systems. The first is the high investment in resources relative to land production. While hydroponics is usually much cheaper over time, developing some kind of more extensive system needs a significant upfront cost. First, there is the possibility of a power failure that can cause pumps to stop their crops from functioning and kill them. Lastly, many people are afraid that hydroponics takes extensive know-how and research, even though it is quite close to conventional gardening. After all, to grow, plants rely on specific nutrients, and these nutrients do not change, regardless of the method you use.

Benefits and Disadvantage of Hydroponics System

Hydroponics is a system of growing plants, herbs, and fruit in a solution that is water-based and rich in nutrients without soil. A grower needs to be very experienced when growing plants in the ground to know how much water he has to give his plants. Too much and the roots of the plant were not capable of having enough oxygen, and the plant will dry up and die. You need to know the proper knowledge about this that how it works, is it beneficial or not for you so, here are we listed some advantages and disadvantages of this system so you can understand this better.

List of Benefits

One of the most significant benefits that hydroponics has over soil growth is the availability of energy. A grower has to be very experienced when growing plants in the soil to know how much water he has to give his plants. Too much and the roots of the plant are incapable of having enough oxygen. Too low, and the plant will dry out and die. Hydroponics addresses this problem in many ways.

Make better use of space:

Since everything that plants need is given and maintained systematically, you can develop in your small apartment as long as you have some space.

The roots of plants typically grow and spread in search of food, and in soil, oxygen. In Hydroponics, roots are submerged in full tank of oxygenated nutrient solution and close contact with essential minerals; this is not so. This means you can grow far closer to your plants, and thereby save huge energy.

No Soils Needed:

In a way, crops can be grown in areas where the soil is restricted, non-existent, or highly polluted. Hydroponics was widely used in the

1940s to supply fresh vegetables for troops in Wake Island, a Pan American airline refueling stop. This is a small region of Pacific Ocean arable. Hydroponics was also considered by NASA as the potential farming to cultivate food for astronauts in space (where no soil exists).

Climate control:

As in greenhouses, farmers may have complete climate control-humidity, temperature, light intensification, air composition. In that sense, no matter the season, you can grow food all year round. To order to increase their business income, farmers should grow food at the right time.

Climate control:

As in greenhouses, hydroponic farmers may have complete climate control-humidity, temperature, light intensification, air composition. In that sense, no matter the season, you can grow food all year round. To order to increase their business income, farmers should grow food at the right time.

Efficient use of nutrients:

In Hydroponics, you have control over the nutrients (foods) required by plants. Before planting, growers should test what plants need and how much nutrients they need at different levels, and combine them with water. Nutrients are conserved in the tank, and there are no nutrient losses or shifts as they are in the soil.

Solution control pH:

All minerals are in the water. This ensures this compared to soils; you can calculate and change the pH levels of the mixture of water much better. That ensures the optimum uptake of plant nutrients.

Good growth rate:

 Are plants increasing faster hydroponically than in soil? Indeed, it is. You are your boss, who controls the entire ecosystem for the growth of your plants-temperature, light, moisture, and nutrients in particular. Plants are put in optimal conditions, while nutrients are supplied in adequate amounts, and the root systems come into direct contact. Thus, plants no longer spend precious energy checking the soil for diluted nutrients. Then, they turn their entire emphasis on growing and processing fruit.

Hydroponics is water-saving:

Hydroponic plants can only use 10 percent of water relative to field-grown plants. This process recirculates the water. Plants will take the water they need, while the run-off ones will be caught and returned to the network. Water loss happens only in two cases-evaporation and system leakage (but the effective hydroponic design can reduce or have no leakage).

Agriculture is expected to use up to 80 percent of land and surface water in the United States. Although water will become a critical problem in the future as the FAQ predicts that food production will increase by 70 percent, Hydroponics is considered a feasible option for large-scale food production.

No weeds:

If you've grown up in the dirt, you'll understand how annoying weeds make your garden look. For gardeners, it is the most time-consuming activities-till, plow, hoe, etc. Weeds are mainly soil related. So clear the nutrients, and all weed bodies are gone.

More insecticide use, and herbicides:

Because you don't use nutrients, so while weeds, pests, so plant diseases are significantly reduced, fewer pesticides are used. That helps you grow safer and cleaner foods. Insecticide and herbicide cutting is a valid point of Hydroponics as the standards for modern life, and food protection is gradually being put on top of it.

List of Disadvantages

It seems as though there's nothing wrong with hydroponics, with all these advantages! Not exactly true. Soil serves as a buffer for increasing errors-errors that are much more costly in hydroponics and can destroy a whole crop. Furthermore, higher humidity levels are welcoming fungi and mildew into the environment, which can kill a crop. Here is a list of disadvantages of hydroponics you should keep in mind.

1. A Hydroponic Garden Needs Your Time And Commitment:

Like all things that are worth living, a hard-working and conscientious attitude produces satisfactory results. Nevertheless, plants can be left alone for days and weeks in soil-borne equivalents and still thrive in a short time. Mother Nature and soils can continue to control when anything balances. In Hydroponics, this is not the case. Plants will die out faster, without proper treatment and awareness. Remember that for their survival, your plants rely on you. Upon initial deployment, you will take good care of your plants and the system. You can then automate this later, but you still need to gage and avoid the operations ' unforeseen problems and do regular maintenance.

2. Technical knowledge:

You operate a network with several types of equipment that need a special experience for the instruments you use, which plants you can develop, and how they will survive and flourish in a soilless setting. Faults in setting up the growth potential of the systems and plants in this soilless atmosphere, and you end up losing your entire development.

3. Natural debates:

There were several intense disputes as to whether or not Hydroponics would be accredited as sustainable. People doubt whether hydroponically grown plants can obtain microbiomes as are in soil. But people have been growing hydroponic plants for tens of years-lettuces, tomatoes, strawberries, etc., particularly in Australia, Tokyo, the Netherlands, and the United States. They provided food for hundreds of people. You can't expect anything in life to be fine. Compared with Hydroponics, there are also more threats of toxins, pests, etc. for soil increasing. For Hydroponic crops, there are several suggested organic growing methods. For example, by using natural growing medium such as coco coir, some growers provide plant microbiomes and add worm casting into it. Nature or organic nutrients, such as fish, bones, alfalfas, cotton seeds, neems, etc., are widely used. Work is still being done for this debate on the organic food problem at the moment and shortly. Until then, we'll know the reaction.

4. Water and energy risks:

Often you use water and electricity in a hydroponic method. Beware of electricity near a mixture of vapor. Working with the water systems and electrical equipment, particularly in commercial greenhouses, often put safety first.

5. Device malfunction threats:

You are operating the entire machine using electricity. So suppose you don't take preventive action for a power outage, the system will immediately stop working, and plants will dry out quickly and die in several hours. Therefore, a backup power source and plan should always be prepared, particularly for systems of great scale.

6. Initial expenses:

You're likely to invest less than one hundred to a few hundred dollars (depending on the size of your garden) to buy equipment for your first setup. You'll need containers, lamps, a pump, nutrient, growing media, timer whatever systems you build). When the system is in operation, only electricity and nutrients can minimize the cost.

7. High return:

If you follow news about the start-up of agriculture, you might have learned that some new hydroponic indoor business has recently begun. That's also good for the agriculture sector and Hydroponics production.

Large scale Hydroponics. This is due in large part to the high initial costs and the long, unpredictable ROI (return on investment). A simple profitable strategy to encourage investment is not easy to describe. However, there are also several other attractive high-tech fields out there that seem to be relatively promising for financing.

CHAPTER 2
GETTING STARTED:
WHAT DO YOU NEED?

Generally speaking, hydroponics will be as complex or as simple as you make it. Some of the methods you have been introduced do have more stringent requirements, but for the most part, so long as you have a few simple pieces of equipment, you can ensure your system will be up and running before long.

We are going to go over every one of the basic requirements that you will need to meet to ensure that you can get your system up and running with ease. If you can follow these recommendations, you should find that ultimately, your system will work well. Make sure you weigh what you need versus what you can afford. However, for the most part, you can come up with a highly affordable option that will allow you to make use of these systems yourself.

The Reservoir

This is the most fundamental part that you are going to need. This is where you are going to store your nutrient solution for your plant. Sometimes, your plants will be suspended into this, and other times, it will simply pump throughout the system, depending upon the methods you are using. It will be up to you to figure out which method you are going to use to ensure you get the proper size.

Generally speaking, your reservoir should drain no more than 20% per week. This is to ensure that you do not accidentally wind up with some degree of imbalance in nutrients, which can absolutely devastate your system if it is not taken care of properly. Rather than running the risk of your system being out of balance as certain nutrients are absorbed quicker than others, you should instead make it a point to aim bigger.

To help you make your informed decision, try to keep in mind that small plants usually require roughly ½ of a gallon per plant on the system. Medium plants will require around 1 ½ gallon per plant, and larger plants will need at the very least 2 1/2 gallons of water, though there is a good chance a very large plant will require more.

Think of this as a minimum size—you may want to get something larger if you have the space to do so. Try to keep in mind that you use an inert material for your reservoir, but if all you have is a plastic bucket, that is better than nothing at all.

The Grow Tray

This will vary greatly from person to person. The grow tray will be where your plants are suspended and growing. Some methods will make use of a PVC pipe, or a gutter for the grow tray, while others will require the use of a legitimate tray of sorts. You will ultimately need to pick one large enough for the system you are designing and will give the plants you have chosen ample space to ensure everything is going to grow properly. The grow tray will most often have several net pots within it to hold onto the plants and keep them in the right position.

The Lighting

Lighting is one of the most crucial parts of any indoor grow operation. You need to be certain that the growth that you are doing is going to have the right amount of light, and that means that you are going to have to invest. The sun has a very specific kind of light that it produces—it can create the whole spectrum, which is what plants need. However, most indoor lights are not capable of producing this. Because of this, you are going to want to invest in good lighting if you are going to be growing on larger scales.

If you are just growing for your family as a hobby, you should be fine with just the spectrum from fluorescent light for most plants. However, if you want to see major amounts of crops produced, you will need to use good, high-quality lighting for your system to function properly and get the growth that good hydroponics systems are known for.

If you are short on money, however, you can stretch your budget by using several light reflectors. These will allow you to spread the light you are already producing further just by reflecting it further. When you can spread the lighting further, you can get the light to more of the plants without having to buy another light.

Make sure you always research your plants and their need for light as well—some plants will require more or less light, and that can lead to all sorts of discrepancies. If you try to give a plant too much light, you run the risk of it overgrowing or growing incorrectly. Without enough light, your plant cannot produce the energy it needs to thrive. You need to find that happy medium, which varies from plant to plant.

The Air Pump

Your air pump is not going to vary much from system to system. You will need to make sure that you have a pump that is strong enough to aerate your system. Usually, the pumps you can buy at a fish store will be just fine for this, and they usually come in several different prices. When you remember this, you will then be able to produce better plants in general. If you are not making sure that your water is oxygenated enough, your plants are not going to be able to absorb enough. This is particularly important for deepwater systems—if your water is not being circulated around, it is not going to have enough oxygen in it, and the plants, if their roots are entirely submerged, are going to die.

You may find you will need more than one air pump if you want a system that is going to be larger, and that is okay. All that matters is you get ones that will produce bubbles and have a decently sized air stone to go along with them.

The Water Pump

Your water pump is going to be one of the most important parts of most of these systems. If you do not get the right one, or if you get a cheap one that cannot pump enough, your system is going to fail. Most water pumps will work for smaller-scale operations. But if you are trying to pump water through a larger system, or you have to pump water up particularly high into a system, such as with a tower build, you may need to invest in a more expensive, and therefore, more powerful build.

Keep in mind you do not want to skimp here. Your pump is going to be giving your plants the nourishment they need. It is like the heart, pumping the nutrients throughout the system so it can continue to flourish and thrive.

The pump you get can be complex in some ways—some will come with timers and adjusters built into them. Others, however, are more bare-bones and will simply pump water. The one you get will be dependent upon your needs. Some considerations for your water system include:

- Do you want a pump that is submerged or one that is external?
- Does it have the features that you want?
- Does it pump enough for the system you are building?
- Does it seem reliable?

The Timer

The timer is crucial if you want to save time or if you want to make use of an ebb and flow system. When you are using a system like this, you will need the water to be released at certain times for certain amounts of time. You want to ensure the timer you are making use of is going to provide these functions for you. This means you will want to ensure you can turn off and on as necessary.

Some timers can provide you with a bit more flexibility. They can be programmed to turn on and off several components at different times. Others are very simple and will shut off or on at regular points in time to change up how they are working for you.

When you make use of these systems, you will really just be saving yourself time, however, and many of the different methods of gardening do not even require these at all. If you, for example, are going to be growing a garden with a deep water method, you are not going to need a timer unless you do not want to have to worry about the timers. If your system is not timer-dependent, then this may be a great way for you to save some money.

The Growth Medium

Growth medium is largely all the same. It will all provide you with the same benefits—it is inert, so it does not react to the plants or provide any nutrients. However, sometimes, you can find the medium can absorb the nutrients that were provided in the water that goes over them. You may want to do this to allow your medium to hold onto the liquid, like using a wick system. Sometimes, you will not be using a growth medium at all, such as when your plants are going to be entirely submerged into the system, like with a deep water culture. This will be mostly dependent upon your preferences, and you should be able to find something that is going to work for you and your system relatively easily.

Some of the most common growth mediums you can choose from include:

- Vermiculite
- Perlite
- Expanded clay
- Coco coir
- Rock wool
- The Monitoring Equipment

Finally, you must get your monitoring equipment as well. This will primarily happen with a pH tester and an EC monitor. The pH refers to the acidity or alkalinity of your system. It is required that you will have your system within the proper pH requirements for the plants you are looking for. Because of this, you will be able to check the pH on a regular basis whenever you are altering the water in any way, as well as on a regular basis before and after adding water in the first place. You can adjust the pH of your water if it is not where it is supposed to be.

The other main piece of equipment you will need will be an EC meter. This will read the ionization of the solution you are using in your system, allowing you to figure out the concentration of your solution to ensure it is right where it is supposed to be. This system works by measuring the electrical conductivity within the system that you are using to determine whether or not it is going to be balanced out. If it is too concentrated, then you have to dilute it down further. If it is not concentrated enough, you will need to add more.

Because you need to keep your system in tip-top condition to prevent problems with your plants, this is a very important part of your arsenal. However, these are typically relatively low-cost and should all yield the same results for your system, no matter the testing equipment you may have.

CHAPTER 3
HOW TO BUILD YOUR OWN HYDROPONIC SYSTEM

We know to build your hydroponic system is an arduous task to do. And especially if you have no experience and technical knowledge about the system, then it seems like an impossible task. But seriously there is nothing like impossible thing in building the hydroponic system because you only need to follow some simple steps and then you will get your hydroponic system without any error.

1) Determine the space/location

Indeed, one of the most essential and initial steps for building your hydroponic system. An excellent place or space where you want to establish your system is the path of attaining success. It doesn't matter whether you are developing your hydroponic system in your home or outside your home or in an open space area, the place should be levelled to maintain the right balance of the system.

If you are planning to locate the hydroponic system inside your home, then choose a dry place and a place which is far away from the electrical circuit. Though some of the systems run on electricity, you also need to remember that water will also be present in the system and any leakage can cause severe damage.

And if you want to locate your hydroponic system outside, then you have to must ensure the prevention of your network from outside elements like wind barrier, temperature and humidity level, protection from worms and other pests. And in the cold temperature, you need to bring your system inside your home to prevent the plants.

2) Assemble - Hydroponic System

Each hydroponic system has a specific design and structure. Some are highly equipped because of their commercial purpose, and some are like a wicking system which mainly made for house farming.

So, let's know about general hydroponic systems assemble process:

Your hydroponic system consists of with reservoir that is also known as container or tank, the tubes through which water and solution come, net pot or anything which holds the plants, water pump and stone which creates the bubbles, recycle the water and generate enough oxygen for the plants. Some other essential things like nutrients solutions. So, after getting all these things, then assemble them carefully.

3) Mixing of the nutrient solution in the tank

Then fill up the tank with water. And after that add some needed amount of nutrients into the tub and turn on the pump so that water and nutrients solution will mix thoroughly.

4) Add Plants

If you do not have any experience or time to grow seeds by yourself, then it would be best for you to purchase seeds from the market, and this is the most-simplest process of planting a hydroponic garden. But for more significant results, you need to choose a healthier plant root of your desire and then clean it thoroughly. It means to remove all the soil and dirt from the sources.

After that wash them gently and submerge the roots into the lukewarm water to cold water. Remember that too cold or hot water can damage the roots and give them initial shock that can cause unhealthier results. And then separate each root for removing the soil because any soil left can log the spray holes.

So, after cleaning the roots, pull the roots from the bottom of the cup of planting and add some stretched clay pebbles. These clay are hard and capable enough to hold the roots without any damage.

5) Tie the sources in the trellis

The next step involves the process of attaching the origins in the grille. For this, you can use strings and plant clips to tie the plant's roots to the trellis, because chains and clips can attain better support for the plant. And these are also helpful in maximizing the space. So, tie up the strings to the top of the roots through a grille. Then, attach the clips at the bottom of the plant.

6) Turn the system on and monitor it

We are saying because sometimes due to the evaporation or excessive heat, the system runs out of the water and in that particular situation the tank become dry and your pump can burn up too.

On the other hand, you also need to check the nutrients level and PH level in a regular interval of time.

7) Measure plant growth

Hydroponic farming or planting is the most significant way of getting quick and better results. Because the plant needs water and nutrients for overgrowing and through a hydroponic system, they consume it more rapidly. They grow faster, and that is why you need to monitor or measure plant growth every day.

8) Check the diseases and pests in the plant

Disease and pests are one of the biggest obstacles in the process of hydroponics. Any bug or pests can destroy your hard work in a short period. Any foliar disease chewed leaves, and insect pest presence can damage your entire system.

So, it would be better for you to remove plant which is infected or sick immediately. Plants that grow hydroponically do not need to spend their energy to locate food because they automatically get the required food. That is why they spend their strengths to fight with the disease and with any infection.

Essentiality of hydroponic farming

1) Soilless growing

The story of hydroponic growing was started in 1940 when some researchers had introduced the phenomenon of the hydroponic system by growing vegetables without soil for the American troops. It was indeed a great and successful experiment in science. And now we all have been watching and gaining the benefits of landless growing or tank-based growing.

The most significant benefits of this method are that now we can grow plants and do farming where the soil is not appropriate for agriculture and gardening.

2) Space friendly

Yes, you can step up your hydroponic system wherever you want and can get some outstanding results of plantation or agriculture. If you wish to locate your order on the outside of your home or inside, it will give you the same results. Though you need to take care of some points like prevention from dirt and dust or faster wind because these can erupt the smooth progress of growing.

3) Control over climate conditions

The tradition farming or plantation mainly depends on the weather conditions and shows the growth according to the climate and seasons. That is why we get the vegetables and fruits available in the market according to the seasons.

But, here the all process will be done on the tank or reservoir. It means you have total control over climate, seasons, weather conditions and air, temperature, and humidity. So, you can grow plants according to your need and also earn some high amount commercially.

4) Can save more water

Traditional farming or plantation requires more water consumption, and this is one of the biggest reasons why ground-level water degrading so much. A data says traditional farming method consumes around 80 percent of water in comparison to soilless growing.

And if we talk about the hydroponic way, then it would be around 10 percent of water consumption. So, in this way, you can be able to save more water. Because there is only one way of water wasting in hydroponic and that is a leakage in the tank.

5) Maximum use of nutrients

Water and nutrients are the main elements which help the plant or roots to be healthy and multiply. But in the traditional method, the plant root takes more time and consumes fewer nutrients in comparison to soilless growing. The hydroponic system method shows the maximized use of the nutrient solution and water for the plant's growth.

By the hydroponic way, you can directly increase the water and nutrients into the roots of a plant, and by this, they will grow healthier and quicker.

6) PH control

Another great benefit of tank based growing in comparison of soil-based growing. Because here we can easily control the PH level of water and nutrients solutions more precisely and also can adjust them. And in this way, we can be able to ensure the number of nutrients consumed in the plant.

7) Greater growth rate

By giving the right atmosphere and climate condition, better nutrient, water supply, and light, you can quickly grow more plants than the traditional method.

And hydroponics is the best way to provide a direct supply of mixed water and nutrient solution. And it is easily understandable that if you are providing all these things, then your growth rate will quickly become higher.

8) No Weed phenomenon

Yes, you heard it right. Because weeds develop in the soil and when you grow your plants hydroponically, then the aspect of weeds will be eradicated automatically. It means you can build your plants and do farming without any stress of weeds.

Because, while doing the soil-based farming, we need to cut down the developed weeds from the soil to prevent the healthier growth of plants.

9) Prevention from diseases

Plant diseases such as fusarium, Pythium, and Rhizoctonia species destroys the healthiness of the plant and make them vulnerable. And pests such as groundhogs and gophers can also do severe damage in the plant growing.

But if you are doing your farming through the tank method, then the chances of these things will be mitigated automatically.

10) Time-saving

In comparison to the traditional approach, you can save your significant amount of time through hydroponic farming. In the conventional method, you need to devote your time for watering, soil cultivation, and monitoring, but here you need to understand the equipment of tank based farming. And the rest will be done by the system itself. By this, you can be able to save your time and your labor too.

11) Stress-free work

Indeed, it is a stress-free way of doing farming of gardening. There is no need to do the soil cultivation or watering for the better soil condition. And you also need not devote your significant amount of time. However, you can do hydroponic farming as a hobby to make your life stress free.

CHAPTER 4

HOW TO MAKE THE MOST OUT OF YOUR HYDROPONIC GARDEN

Know the Equipment You Need and Why

Before you go shopping for your kit, make a list of what you need and understand why you need each item. It will help ensure you get the right things and keep your budget under control.

Know What Food Your Plants Need

You must know how to dilute the nutrients, measure its strength and the pH level of the solution too. Don't worry, if this sounds like you need a degree in chemistry; it is very simple, and most of the measurements can be done with machines where you press a button, it beeps and then gives you a reading! Do remember that some plants are greedier than others and so will need more food. Lettuce, for example, isn't a particularly hungry plant whereas tomatoes like plenty of food to produce a healthy crop.

Know the Light Requirements of Your Plants

Different plants prefer different amounts of light. This means you either need to come to a compromise if you are growing a variety of plants where some will not have ideal conditions, or you need to have a separate setup for each type of plant, which can be expensive. Try growing plants that have similar light and nutrient requirements together as they will thrive. If you grow plants that have wildly different needs together in one growing environment, then you can find the plants get ill and struggle to produce a crop.

Use A 3-Part Nutrient Product

There are one and two-part nutrient products out there, but the three-part ones provide the best results in a long way. They allow you to get the balance right for your plants during their stages of growth and are generally much easier to use. Just remember to add the parts one at a time and mix thoroughly between each addition.

Don't Use Nutrient Additives at First

It is tempting to throw some nutrient additives into the mix with the belief that it will do your plants some good. In all likelihood, it will not, and experienced growers will only use nutrient additives if there is a problem with their plants or the plants they are growing have very specific requirements.

Keep the Light Ballast Units Elsewhere

These ballast units give off a lot of heat which can affect the growth of your plants and encourage pests, diseases and even the formation of algae. Keep these units elsewhere, ideally somewhere with good air circulation to remove the heat from the units. Of course, if you are using LED lighting, you will not have an issue with ballast units

Monitor and Adjust Your Nutrient Reservoir Regularly

This is very important to ensure that your plants are getting the optimal level of nutrients. It can very easily become stronger or weaker as your plants absorb more food or water, which will impact their growth. Stressed plants become more susceptible to disease, so check the strength daily at around the same time every day and then adjust the solution every couple of days as required

Minimize Exposure to Light for Your Nutrient Solution

Ideally, you want your nutrient reservoir to be dark or at least wrap it in dark paper or something so that light cannot get into it. This is why black tubing is preferred for all connections, to stop the light from getting to the nutrient solution. When it is exposed to light, algae get the energy to grow and will soon take over your hydroponic system. By keeping light exposure to a minimum, you will slow the growth of algae and prevent clogging. Most importantly, it reduces the amount of work you have to do cleaning and maintaining your system!

Get Your Reservoir Change Water Ready the Day Before

When you change your reservoir water, the freshwater needs to be left out for the chlorine to evaporate for a period of 12 to 24 hours. Get the water ready the day before and then, when you come to change your nutrient reservoir, the water does not need to sit around, and you can do it immediately.

Change the Nutrient Solution Regularly

You need to change the nutrient solution once every one or two weeks. After this time algae may start to grow in it, and the nutrient solution itself will be weaker. As you measure the nutrient solution daily, you will know when it needs a change. If your hydroponic system is somewhere that gets a lot of light, then you want to change the solution closer to the week mark to prevent algae build-up.

Clean and Sterilize EVERYTHING Between Crops

This is vital to prevent the build-up of bacteria, pests and other contaminants in your system. Scrub everything well. Flush hoses and your spray nozzles need thoroughly cleaning too. Ensure that everything is well rinsed and there is no disinfectant residue on it when you set the system back up again, as this could damage your plants.

Don't Go Straight into Your Hydroponic Garden After Being Outside

Before going into your hydroponic garden, make sure you at least change your shoes. In larger setups, you may want to change your clothes as well or put on an overall that is only worn in the hydroponic environment. This will prevent pests, diseases and fungal spores being brought in on your clothing or shoes and then introduced into your growing environment. Most diseases and fungal spores are microscopic, meaning you will not be able to see if you have any on you. This is a simple precaution to take, which will prevent problems for your plants.

No Pets Allowed

Again, this is common sense; pets are covered in microscopic debris from outside, particularly dogs, which they can then transfer into your hydroponic garden. Cats are far too curious and will sit on your plants, eat them or otherwise cause major disruption to your hydroponic growing environment. They can very easily damage something or introduce pollutants into the system.

Ensure Visitors Follow These Rules

If you are showing anyone your hydroponic garden, then make sure they follow these same rules as it will ensure they do not introduce a problem into your garden.

CHAPTER 5

DO IT YOURSELF:

FROM SEEDS TO HARVEST

How To Start Seeds

The best way to start seeds is to use a seed starter cube. A cube the size of one and a half inch will fit perfectly in a two-inch net pot. These small cubes are capable of holding water while air can reach the roots, which is the most important while germinating seeds.

First, you need to soak your grow cubes in chlorine or chloramine free water with a pH of 5.5. Water from your tap will be around 7-8 pH. You most likely need to use a pH down solution.

Getting the chlorine out of your tap water is quite easy. Let it sit for one day for the chlorine to evaporate. If you want it to evaporate faster, you can use an air stone to air the chlorine out much quicker.

If your water company uses chloramine, you need a reverse osmosis filter to remove the chloramine. Note that not every reverse osmosis filter can remove chloramine. Chloramine can't be aired out and needs to be filtered. If you do not have a reverse osmosis filter available, you can use one thousand mg (one gram) of vitamin C (ascorbic acid) per forty gallons (one hundred and fifty liters) of water.

Use a tray to soak the cubes, pour the water on top, and let it sit for a few minutes. Once most of the water is absorbed, you need to drain the rest of the water. Do not squeeze the cubes. This will remove air pockets inside the cubes.

The next step is dropping your seeds into the holes. This can be a big task if you need to do a lot of seeds. Commercial growers use pelleted seeds and a vacuum seeder to speed this process up. Pelleted seed is a seed that is wrapped in clay. it is bigger, thus easier to handle.

You could also use a toothpick and dip the tip in some water. This will make the seed stick to the toothpick, as shown in the following image.

Using a wet toothpick to pick up seeds

Placing the seed into the seed starter cube

If the holes of the grow media are preventing you from dropping the seed in, use pen or toothpick to open the hole back up.

You can use more than one seed per hole if the germination rate is terrible. I always use two seeds per hole. When both seeds germinate, I keep the best one and use scissors to remove the bad one.

Next, place your humidity dome on top of the tray to keep the seed starter cubes moist. Generally, the seeds don't need water until they have germinated. If you notice that your seed starter cubes are drying out, you can pour some more water in the tray. Don't forget to drain the rest of the water.

Once the seeds start showing its first two leaves, you need to put it under a light source. This will provide the plant with the energy they need to grow. If you experience that the stems are growing long (stretching). It means that your plant is reaching for the light. Increase the light on the seedlings to avoid this stretching. Do not use red lights on seedlings. White fluorescents that are 6500K are perfect.

After ten days, you can transplant them to your system. If you are growing in a greenhouse, it can take fifteen days in winter.

Heat mats will increase germination during colder weather. The mats are placed under the seedling tray to warm up the seed starting cubes. Setting the heat mat to 68°F is recommended.

Recap:

1. Soak your seed starting cubes in chlorine or chloramine free water. Distilled water is even better. Make sure the pH is around 5.5.

2. Put the seed starting cubes in a tray.

3. Put the seed in the holes of the seed starter cubes.

4. Cover the seed starting cubes with a humidity dome.

5. Set the heat mat to 68°F (20°C) and place it under the tray.

6. Once sprouts appear, water them from the bottom with one quarter nutrient strength. The cubes will wick up the water.

7. Place them under T5 fluorescent lights. The humidity dome is still on the tray.

8. When you see four leaves and the roots are developing out of the seed starting cubes, it is time to transplant them to your growing system.

8.2 Seedling Stage

Once your seedling has become strong enough, they can be transplanted into the hydroponic growing media. In general, once your seedling has produced a couple of true leaves, it is ready to be transplanted. The true leaves won't be the first leaves the plant forms. The first one to three leaves is known as cotyledons. The true leaves come after those and are often larger and darker.

When you transplant, you want to make sure that the growing media is supporting the plant so that it sits upright and is stable. The roots need to be completely covered so that they will be in the nutrient mixture.

8.3 Vegetative Stage

Once your plant is in your hydroponic system, you have to make sure that it has everything it needs. That means you need to check the pH and everything of your nutrient solution to make sure it is getting the nutrients and oxygen that it needs. Also, make sure that you are keeping up with the correct lighting schedule for your plant. It's the first few weeks of life in your system that are the most important. They can make or break your plant.

There is something that you have to keep an eye on during your plant's entire life, and those are pests. You may be wondering how hydroponic plants that are grown inside could face pests, but they do. If you don't prepare yourself for them, an infestation could undo all of your hard work. Let's take some time to discuss pests and how to prevent them from infesting your hydroponic plants.

8.4 Flowering Stage

Some plants will require pollination for them to produce their vegetable. There are some plants that self pollinate, and you won't have to worry about pollination. Something that people may take for granted when growing plants is when they are grown outside in a regular garden is that bees or butterflies and other animals naturally pollinate your plants.

When the plant is brought inside into a hydroponic system, you no longer have natural pollinators working for you. To some degree, you may have some natural pollination with the movement of air, vibration, or shaking when plants are pruned or trained, but you can't count on that.

How to pollinate plants will all depend on the plant itself. The majority of fruit-bearing species will require some type of pollination, with the one exception being commercial hydroponic cucumbers, which exhibit a parthenocarpy fruit set. Eggplants, peppers, strawberries, melons, and tomatoes will all benefit from some pollination assistance.

Luckily, this won't involve precise work, at least for the most part. The most common type of pollination is hand pollination. It is very efficient, cheap, and flexible. The main thing you have to think about is timing. Pollen on the flower is only viable for a very short period, and flowers tend to open quickly under the right growing conditions, so you have a very small window to do this. When it comes to self-pollinating plants such as peppers and tomatoes, hand pollination only requires flicking, shaking, or tapping the behind the flowering truss or the flower.

The rapid but gentle movement of the flower will release the pollen from the flower anthers. It will look like a cloud of yellow dust. Once it has been released, the pollen will fall onto the stigma and will start to germinate. The pollen tube will grow into the style, and the fertilization process will occur after a few hours. Fertilization of your plant's flower will result in the creation of seeds. In plants like peppers and tomatoes, the number of seeds and the growth hormone that it releases will determine how big the fruit gets.

When it comes to fruiting crops like melons, hand pollination can become more complex. These plants grow male and female flowers and the pollen from the male flower has to be transferred to the female flower. You will have to pluck the male flowers from the plant, strip back the petals, and their stamen has to be wiped over the stigma of the female flowers.

Male flowers will start being produced weeks before the plant starts producing female flowers, so you will have to be patient. You can differentiate the two because the female flower will have a small, green fruitlet, or egg, at the base of the flower. Not every hand-pollinated flower will set and grow. It is very common for some of your fruitlet to turn yellow, wither, and fall off. This is perfectly normal and helps prevent the plant from producing more fruit than it will be able to support. This is why vining plants, like melons and pumpkins, will produce a lot of flowers but not nearly as many fruits.

Lastly, you can use artificial wind pollination on some plants. Crops like strawberries, which are mainly self-pollinating, benefit from the assistance of the artificial wind. All this will involve is moving large air blowers over the crop rows at the height of the plant after they have started to form flowers. You can do this on small hydroponic systems with a hairdryer set to cool.

8.5 Harvest Stage And Crops

Once your plant has grown its fruit or vegetable, you get to harvest it just like you would with a regular garden. Now, there is one exception to this. If you do any research on hydroponic harvesting, you will come across harvesting hydroponic lettuce.

You have two choices when it comes to harvesting lettuce. One is with roots, and the other is without roots. To harvest with roots, get containers for the lettuce ready and wash your hands. Mist your plants with some freshwater before and during the harvesting. Gently hold onto the lettuce and lift it out of the hydroponic solution. Let the solution drain away and then place the lettuce in the container. Lettuce the roots attached will last you for two to three weeks.

To harvest without the roots, you will simply harvest a few leaves. Mist your lettuce with water beforehand. Make sure that you harvest your lettuce in the morning because the leaves will be more hydrated. Clean off a knife or a pair of scissors. Get a container ready for the cut lettuce. Cut off individual leaves of your lettuce from the outside, and leave the center leaves so that it can continue to grow. Make sure you handle the plant carefully so that it doesn't bruise the other leaves.

Alternatively, you can simply cut the entire plant off at the base with a knife, making sure that the leaves stay attached to the stem.

Congratulations, you have just grown your first plant in a hydroponic garden.

CHAPTER 6

HOW TO MAINTAIN YOUR HYDROPONIC GARDEN

Make Sure It Is Always Clean

Before starting, make sure all your equipments are clean. Your plant box, for example, should be cleaned using a ten percent bleach solution. Whenever there are any dead parts of a plant, make sure they are cut off as soon as possible. When an organic matter starts decaying, it may attract the growth of fungus gnats. Swiftly get rid of plants when you realize they are diseased, else, the infection may spread.

During water change in the reservoir, use a ten percent bleach solution to clean the tank before replacing the water.

Your slabs or big trays should also be washed, especially when you've had to deal with a root tot problem.

Drippers

This is for growers who use the drip system. You should get extra drippers and keep them handy so that you can easily replace clogged up ones. Also, keep vinegar around in your grow room, and have your drippers thrown in it when they get clogged; this is done to clean them up.

Ebb Systems

For the growers that work with the ebb system, get a timer to help you monitor the cycles and water supply to your plants. One cycle should not get the stone wool soaked for more than ten minutes.

Sometimes in your system, you may experience salt build-up. To avoid this, topwater the plants with the same solution that is in the reservoir once a week. If you use plain water, your plant will experience a shock.

Have a tray that has deep grooves that make it easier for water to drain from the GRODAN cubes or slabs.

PH

Always keep a close eye on the Ph of your reservoir, test this before supplying to your hydroponic system. The pH is the alkalinity or acidity levels of water and can be monitored in a lot of ways. The scale runs between 0.0 to 14.0.

- 7.0 means that the pH is neutral; above 7.0 means that it is alkaline

- below 7.0 means, it is acidic.

Typically, plants do well in pH levels between 5.5 to 6.5, but these levels are ultimately defined by the grower and the kind of plants that are grown. Different nutrients get absorbed at different rates, and the pH required can fluctuate depending on the stage the plants are on in their cycle too.

Generally, pH that is below 5 is harmful and may ruin the stone wool. PH above 7 is also an issue, and both levels below five and above seven may make it difficult for the plant to take nutrients up easily.

Before planting your crops, take time, say two hours, to saturate the stone wool with water that has a 5.5 pH.

Also, flush the GRODAN with the 5.5 solution before putting the GRODAN in the system.

Note that when the plant is in its vegetative growth phase, the pH of the system goes up. This is normal and shouldn't frighten you. Most of the time, it's an indication that your plant is doing well and growing. However, there is a need for you to pay attention to the details because sometimes, increased pH could be as a result of the growth of algae or the increase in temperature. Most plants typically do well in a pH of 6.

Reservoir Nutrient Solution

To be on the safe side, replace your nutrient t solution once every week. Topping up the reservoir isn't such a bad idea, but the only problem is that your solution may be infected with root rot or may no longer contain essential micronutrients. If your nutrient solution reservoir contains a diluted solution that is ready for use, lower the pH with the help of lemon juice or phosphoric acid.

Observe and Learn

Pay close attention to your system, and record things like the temperature, pH, EC, light level and carbon dioxide, every day. This will help you see clearly what you're doing wrong and what you're getting right.

If you notice that your plants are not flourishing, go back to your records and find out what the issue might be. Every content must be balanced, nothing lopsided. You can alter parameters slowly, one at a time, to see the results you get.

If the reservoir water temperature is too low, heat up a bit. If flowering and fruiting prove difficult for you and your plants, try increasing the difference between the temperature in the day and the temperature at night. If this also doesn't do, increase the injection of carbon dioxide in the day.

Calcium Deficiency

Always check to make sure your plants aren't deficient. For example, when you notice a downward curl of young leaves, then it may be indicative of a calcium deficiency. If the downward curl happens in older leaves, then the issue may be from the root, which in turn also affects intake of Calcium.

Calcium deficiency occurs when there isn't sufficient movement of water through the plant. Since Calcium travels through the plant's water stream, not the plant's nutrient stream, when it is insufficient, it means it is most likely a climate problem. In high humidity, calcium uptake becomes difficult, even when Calcium is abundant in the nutrient solution. So, it is not a nutrient solution problem.

Huge fluctuations in the humidity of daytime and nighttime may also affect the flow of Calcium through the plant. This could ultimately cause BER (Blossom-End Root). Poor root development could also lead to poor calcium uptake and BER. Roots often develop poorly as a result of a root pathogen known as Pythium or temperatures of low substrates.

The root that is behind the root-tip is the area through which Calcium gets taken up. So, if these new root tips are not formed, the uptake of Calcium is drastically reduced.

Pay Attention to Your Plants

Your plants should be your top priority. Pay attention to their leaf color, their shape, are there bugs? Are they looking perky? Whenever you notice a slight misnomer, fix as early as possible. Also, record everything you notice about then plants so that you have a full picture of the plant's progress or deterioration.

At least every three days, test the balance of nutrients, check water levels and the pH in the solution, to be sure there is no shortage of essential nutrients, pH problem or water problem. There are various ways to check the pH of the solution in the hydroponic system; digital meters, paper test strips and liquid pH test kits. Digital meters are technologically advanced ways of checking pH, with a digital pen as the most popular meter type. The most cost-effective way to check for pH is with the paper test strips, while the popular one used by hobby gardeners is the liquid pH test kit. When you are adding water to your system, add the nutrient solution to it, else you risk diluting the container liquid and ruining the nutrient balance of the system.The plant growth patterns should also not elude you. Whenever you notice that there are diseases or pests, get rid of them fast.

At some point in the growth of plants, especially when they've matured, clip them to help them grow better, and with more vigor.

Once the plants are ripe or mature, harvest them to enable them to produce even more.

Pay attention to the wind and light levels, so that you can easily adjust them when they are too low or too high. To adjust, you can get rid of screen cloth, or find a more protected area for the system, so that your plants don't get damaged. If it is the rainy season, be sure your nutrient levels have not been diluted, as this could affect your plant growth if overlooked.

Be sure the pump is always working and is efficiently supplying the necessary nutrients to the plants. Every three weeks, the nutrient reservoir should be changed, and at given periods, cleanse your system using hydrogen peroxide and clean water so that no build-up could be harmful to the system and so that the piping stays clean.

Advice

Everyone will always have something to say, including your family, friends, and even hobbyists. You mustn't always swallow hook, line and sinker whatever advice you're given. The fact that it worked for Person A doesn't always mean it will work for person X,Y and Z. Your growing conditions are different, and it's best to experience and observe what is best for your plants yourself.

EC

Regardless of the plant, if you want your plants to be healthy, you will have to make sure that the EC levels are sufficient. In EC, the amount of salts dissolved is a measure. It directly and generally correlates to available nutrients. It is, therefore, important that you test the EC levels. There are EC meters used to test EC levels. These meters are placed in the water, and they indicate water conductivity by passing an AC voltage.

Water Temperature

Every hydroponic water temperature is usually between 68 degrees and 72 degrees F. To maintain your temperature; you can make use of water chiller to lower and water heater to increase temperatures. This way, you make sure that the water you're supplying to your plants is not too cold or too hot.

Fertigation System

Fertigation is the process through which fertilizers are injected into an irrigation system. You must pay attention to your fertilizer distribution in water supply, and your plants have nothing else to fall back to if you get the nutrient levels or water levels wrong.

This is unlike the soils that can provide a buffer for acids, bases and salts you may have added to your system. Since the hydroponic system has no buffer, you need to be careful; else your plants may experience chemical shock.

However, admittedly, it isn't as easy to always get the right fertilizer amount. It is complicated, having the fertilizer mix into the water supply, and ensuring that the pH is suitable enough to enable the plants to take in the nutrient solution in exact amounts. Without the fertigation system, you may find it difficult and will have to continue carrying out trials and errors until you arrive at the perfect pH. Fertigation allows for efficiency in your fertilizer supply, leading to stability and better growth of your plants.

You will still have to test the pH levels, but this time, your process will be a lot more accurate. Learn to calibrate your system, at least once every month, to make sure that the fertilizer supplied is done in the right amounts, and that the pH levels are the same as it should be.

It won't take out testing the pH levels. However, it will make it with the goal that the perfect measure of manure is appropriated each time all the more accurately, making the procedure smoother. Cultivators ought to adjust their framework in any event per month, in a perfect world once at regular intervals, to guarantee the perfect measure of manure is being applied, and to ensure pH levels are the place they ought to be.

This is also better when compared with hiring manual labor. You only spend on the fertigation system once and have it serve you for years, unlike manual labor that you keep paying for as long as you need it. Labor costs are currently on the rise so that a fertigation system will save more cost for you in the long run.

Growing Medium

Since there is an absence of soil in the hydroponic system, the plants will need another medium to grow with and be supported by to enable proper nutrient flow through the plants. In the determination of the ideal growing medium, consider the oxygen and moisture balance for easy absorption by the root of the plants.

One common medium is Rockwool. It is commonly used as it is similar to husks gotten from coconuts. It is good with retaining moisture and oxygen and is manufactured in a cube shape so that plants can be placed in rows easily. Rockwool's downside is that you can't use it more than once.

A second medium is the combination of coco coir and clay pebbles, often widely used because of its perfect moisture and oxygen combination. Coco coir is an expensive material gotten from the husks of coconut and clay pebbles are inexpensive clay pellets that can retain oxygen. A mix of both, along with grow rocks, is cost-effective.

Clean Your Hydroponic System Regularly

You can master all of this knowledge and skills, but if you do not learn to keep your hydroponic system clean, all of that knowledge and skill might as well be flushed down the drain. It is by cleaning your hydroponic system regularly that you keep diseases and pests off your plants.

The room in which your plants are grown should be completely sterilized, and your nutrient reservoir should be cleaned at least twice a month. To do this, empty the reservoir and then fill it up, but only halfway, adding some bleach solution (diluted) so that the reservoir can be cleaned effectively. In cleaning, ensure that you observe the reservoir for the build-up of solids, especially in the tubes. Don't also leave out the grow trays or buckets; else you may eventually have to deal with pathogen build-up. Use bleach for them while cleaning and scrub them until they come out spotless, before finally rinsing off. The best time to do this is after each harvest.

You should find the above tips extremely helpful when you start running your own hydroponic system. Ensure the environment of your plants are super-healthy, and they have good water quality. Don't forget fertigation and the ideal growing medium. These among the host of other things I've tackled should guide you on your hydroponic journey.

Fundamental are also the following elements:

Lighting:

Hydroponic systems are usually installed indoor in areas where direct sunlight is not present during the day. Many plants need at least six to seven hours of sunshine each day; even better, 14 to 16 hours. If you have a sunroom or other space with lots of exposed window, supplemental increasing lights are likely to be needed. Hydroponic device kits usually come with the requisite light fixtures, but if you're putting your components together, you'll need to purchase separate light fixtures.

HID as known as High-Intensity Discharge light fixtures are the good source of lighting for a hydroponics device, which may include either HPS (High-Pressure Sodium) or MH (Metal Halide) bulbs. The HPS bulbs emits a red color light, which is perfect for plants in the stage of vegetative growth.

T5 is another form of illumination used in hydroponic rooms. It produces fluorescent, high-output light with low energy consumption. Ideal for that cutting of plants and plants with short growth cycles. Put your lighting device on a timer so that the lights turn on and off every day at the same time.

Water Quality:

Two factors that affect the ability of water to bring nutrients to the plants: the water level of salt minerals as measured by PPM, and the pH of water. Hard water with high mineral content does not remove minerals as easily as water with lower mineral content, so if it is high in mineral content, you may need to filter your water. In a hydroponic device, the optimal pH range for water used is between 5.8 and 6.2 (slightly acid). When the water fails to achieve this standard, chemical substances may be used to change the pH to the optimal range.

Room Conditions:

The setting up of a hydroponic system in the right conditions is quite necessary. Key elements include humidity, temperature, CO2, and airflow. The perfect moisture for a hydroponic growing room is relative humidity from 40 to 60 percent. Higher levels of moisture–particularly in places with poor circulation of air–can lead fungal problems and mildew.

Ideal temperatures range from 68 to 70 degrees Celsius. High temperatures may cause the plants to stunt, and if the temperature of the water is too high, root rot can occur.

There should also be ample supply of carbon dioxide (CO2) in your grow space. The best way to ensure this is by maintaining a continuous airflow in the room. More advanced gardeners of hydroponics should supplement in-room CO2 rates, because the more CO2 will increase the growth of plants.

Nutrients

The used fertilizers in hydroponic systems are available in both liquid and dry, organic, and synthetic types. The substance you are using will contain all the central macronutrients nitrogen, calcium, potassium and magnesium, as well as the essential micronutrients that include trace quantities of manganese, copper, iron, chlorine and zinc.

Using fertilizers designed for hydroponic gardening, if you use them considering the directions of the box, you will get good results. In a hydroponic system, stop using traditional garden fertilizers as their formulations are for use in garden soil.

Select products with hydroponic nutrients that are suited to your particular needs. Others are advertised as better suited for flowering plants, for example, whereas others, like leafy greens, are especially suited to cultivating vegetative growth.

CHAPTER 7

PEST CONTROL

We've made it through setting up our hydroponic garden, picking plants, learning about nutrients and figuring out how we can maintain it. But now we've come across a whole new issue: Pests. Our setup provided an excellent environment for our plants to grow. But it also created an environment which pests love, and we even filled it with tons of healthy plants for them to eat. This would be fine if they provided some kind of service to our plants, but all they want to do is snack on them and leave them wilted and yellowed.

Our number one defense against pests is to prevent them from making our gardens their home in the first place, so we will learn some of the techniques used to detect them early and prevent an infestation.

Pests aren't the only problem we face as hydroponic growers. Disease is also something we must be vigilant in spotting, identifying and handling. To this end, we'll look at some of the more common diseases and how we can prevent them.

Common Hydroponic Pests

While many pests can try to make our gardens their home, certain pests show up with more regularity than others. These pests fall into five key categories: spider mites, thrips, fungus gnats, whiteflies and aphids. If you find yourself with an infestation of pests, it is a safe bet that they'll fall into one of these five categories.

Spider Mites

Out of all five types of pest, spider mites are a particularly annoying one. While they are less than a millimeter long, these little guys are actually tiny spiders. Because they are so small, they tend to start damaging your plants before you even notice that they have taken up in your garden. Spider mite damage will look like tiny brown and yellow spots on the leaves of your plants. While they don't look like anything serious when there are only a couple of bites, this damage adds up quickly to wreak havoc on your garden.

There are two vital signs to look out for to spot a spider mite infestation.

While the damage on your plants can be a telltale sign, it doesn't specifically tell you that spider mites are the problem. To spot a spider mite infestation, you should check your plants to see if you can spot any spider-like webbing. Another way to check for spider mites is to use a tissue or clean rag to wipe the bottoms of your leaves gently. If you come away with streaks of blood, this will tell you that you have a spider mite problem.

One way of handling spider mites is to wash your plants down with a hose or powerful spray bottle. The force of the water can often knock the mites off of your plant and drown them in the growing medium. Spider mites also have some natural enemies ranging from ladybugs to lacewings, and you may consider adding these beneficial insects to your garden to feed on the spider mite population.

Aphids

These little guys are also known as plant lice. And just like head lice, they aren't all that much fun. These tiny, soft-bodied pests are pretty much able to set up in any environment. They multiply quicker than rabbits, so you want to make sure to tackle an aphid infestation as soon as possible. These pests are typically a quarter of an inch in size and can come in green, yellow, pink, black or gray varieties.

Aphids like to feed on the juices of the plant, and you can find them chewing on stems, leaves, buds, fruits or roots. They are particularly drawn to the newest parts of the plant. If you find that your leaves are misshapen or yellowing, checking the bottom can reveal aphids. They also leave behind a sticky substance referred to as honeydew. This sweet substance can actually attract other kinds of pests, so aphids are particularly annoying little critters. This substance can also lead to the growth of fungus, like sooty mold, which can cause your branches or leaves to turn an unpleasant black color. Aphids are also able to carry viruses from one plant to another so they can help nasty pathogens to spread quicker.

Like spider mites, spraying water on the leaves can dislodge them and leave them with a hard time finding their way back to your plants. If the infestation is large, dusting your plants with flour can constipate them and help convince them it is time to move on. Wiping down your plants with a mixture of soapy water can also help to kill and drive them off.

Thrips

Like spider mites and aphids, these little guys are also tiny. Often, they are only around 5 millimetres long. It can be hard to spot these little guys, but they leave damage that is clear as day. If you start to see little metallic black specks on your leaves, you probably have some thrips snacking off your garden. Leaves that thrips attack will often turn brown and become super dry because the thrips like to suck out their juices.

Thrips are small and are either black or the color of straw. They have slender bodies and two pairs of wings. Because they are so small, they look like dark threads to the naked eye. They like to feed in large groups and will fly away if you disturb them. They stick their eggs into flowers and leaves and they only take a couple of days to hatch so a thrip infestation can feel like it just happened out of the blue.

Because thrips like to lay their eggs in plants, it is super important that you remove any dead or fallen plant matter. Make sure that you inspect your plants for thrip damage and remove any that are infested. Hosing off the plants will also help to reduce their population. Ladybugs, lacewings and minute pirate bugs all feed on thrips and can be beneficial to your garden.

Fungus Gnats

Fungus gnats are an odd one. Adult fungus gnats have no interest in harming your garden. But their larvae enjoy chewing on the roots of your plants which slows the growth and opens the plant up for infection. In extreme cases, fungus gnat larvae can cause the death of plants. They really like areas with a lot of moisture and high humidity. You'll likely notice adult fungus gnats before you have any issue. As adults, these gnats are about three millimetres in length and kind of look like mosquitos. They tend to be a grayish-black color with a pair of long legs and clear wings. Their larvae have shiny blackheads with a whitish-transparent body.

Adults typically live for a week and in that time lay up to 300 eggs. It takes half a week for the larvae to emerge, but when they do, they start a two-week diet where their main dish is the roots of your plants. When they feed on your plants, they cause them to wilt, stunt their growth and cause a yellowing of their leaves. These nasty little things can have many generations living off the same plant.

If you suspect a fungus gnat infestation than you should inspect your plants by carefully turning up the soil around their stems and look for larvae, if you check a plant and it suddenly let's loose a bunch of adult gnats then you should dispose of that plant. They like damp soils so make sure you aren't overwatering your plants. If you have a fungus gnat problem you are then letting your potting medium drain longer will help to kill off the larvae and mess up the development of fungus gnat eggs. You can also spray your plants with a combination of peppermint, cinnamon and sesame oils. This mixture is called the flying insect killer and will help to get rid of gnats.

Whiteflies

About the same size as spider mites, whiteflies look like small white moths that take up residence on your plants. They are easier to spot, but because they fly away when you bother them, they can be hard to kill. Like aphids, they enjoy sucking the juices out of your plant, and you see their damage as white spots and yellowing of the leaves.

They tend to lay 200-400 eggs in clusters on the underside of the higher leaves. These eggs hatch in about a week and unattractive little nymphs come out that crawl around on your leaves before they grow wings. These crawlers will spread out from the egg and find a place to start chewing on your leaves. They'll stay in that spot for the next week or so before growing into young adults who will repeat the cycle of movement-feasting.

Ladybugs and lacewings enjoy eating whiteflies and so introducing them to your garden can help to kill off whitefly populations. Hosing off plants with a strong blast of water will help in reducing their numbers as well. There are a bunch of organic pesticides on the market which you can get to deal with whiteflies. These pesticides can also work for the other pests, but pesticides should be a last resort option, one that you are careful with so as not to lead to undue stress on your plants.

Preventing Pests

Now that we have an idea of the pests that are most common to hydroponic gardens let us turn our attention towards how we prevent these pests from getting into our gardens in the first place. Many of these techniques will help us to identify a possible infestation as it is trying to get started and so they offer us early warnings to prepare ourselves to battle pests. If we keep up our preventative measures and keep our eyes peeled for pests, then we can save our plants a lot of damage and ourselves a lot of time by cutting off the problem at the head.

When it comes to pests, it is also important to understand that not every pest is the same. This doesn't just mean that whiteflies are different from fungus gnats. What this means is that fungus gnats on the West coast are going to be different than fungus gnats on the

East coast. Not every solution for prevention or extermination will work. A certain pesticide may be used to kill gnats on the East, but the ones on the West might have grown an immunity to it. For this reason, it is important to check with your local hydroponics store to see if there is any region-specific information you need to tackle your pest problem.

One of the ways that we prevent pests is to make sure that we limit their ability to enter our garden in the first place. We can do this a few ways. Insect screens go a long way to keeping out pests. We also want to limit the amount of traffic in and around our setups. If at all possible, our setups will benefit greatly if airlock entrances can protect them as these offer the most secure protection against both pests and pathogens. Airlocks can be doubled up to create a space before the garden in which to wipe down dirt and any insects or eggs that are catching a free ride on your clothing.

To see if pests are starting to show up in your garden, use sticky traps around your plants. Yellow and blue sticky traps are both useful, as they attract different pests, so you want to make sure to use both kinds for the best results. Place traps near any entrances into your garden, such as doors or ventilation systems. Also, make sure to place one or two near the stems of your plants to catch those pests that prefer snacking on the lower bits, such as aphids or fungus gnats. Get into the habit of checking these traps regularly as they can give you a great idea of what kind of life is calling your garden home.

While traps will help us to get a head start fighting any infections, they aren't a foolproof method when it comes to avoiding pests. Traps should be used together with personal spot checks. This means that you should be checking your plants for pests a couple of times a week. Take a clean cloth and check the bottom of your leaves. Check around the roots for any fungus gnat larvae. You can check the tops of leaves visually. Look for any signs of yellowing or bite marks as described above.

Make sure to remove any weeds that take up root in your garden as these plants are only going to sap your garden's resources and offer a breeding ground for pests. Also remove dead or fallen plant matter, of course. This includes leaves but also any fruit, buds or petals that have been dropped.

Finally, before you introduce any new plants to your garden, make sure to quarantine them first so that you can check them for pests. You can use a magnifying glass to get a closer look if you need to. Give the new plants a thorough inspection, making sure to check all parts of the plant and the potting soil before you transfer it over.

By creating a system and a schedule for inspecting your plants, you can prevent an infestation of pests from ruining your garden or causing you a lot of headaches. A vigilant eye will give you the upper hand in both preventing and dealing with any kind of problem you have with pests. Remember, a strong defence is the best offence when it comes to keeping your plants healthy and free from harm.

CHAPTER 8

HYDROPONIC GARDENING TECHNIQUES

Hydroponics is becoming increasingly common among home gardeners and amateurs of a self-sufficient lifestyle, and for a useful purpose. Within a smaller region, and with much less water, you can produce more vegetables, veggies, and fruits using hydroponic systems than you do use soil-based techniques. You don't have to use any pesticides since you are through in a closed setting. When utilizing conventional approaches, you can be restricted by seasons and agricultural areas; hydroponics lets you opt to sprout anytime you want, wherever you want and wherever you want.

If you're new to the hydroponics universe, the abundance of choices makes it possible to get overwhelmed. We allow the choice more unaffected by differentiating between the schemes, and you can pick the one that fits better for you.

Importance to choose the right method

Owing to the growing need for new, sustainable, and nutritious vegetables, fruits, and other plants that are important in our everyday lives, indoor gardening has gained a lot of popularity worldwide over the past few years.

When done correctly, modern gardening can be satisfying and enjoyable. If you have a free room at home or in the garden, why not pursue hydroponics growing and enjoy a whole year's supply of fresh fruits and vegetables? Not only does this save you a few bucks, but it would also allow your homestead more attractive.

The market today is packed with thousands of hydroponic systems and packages to choose from, and even experts of gardening still find themselves in a bind when selecting the best hydroponics device.

If you're an ambitious gardener, this book offers you a thorough guide on the considerations to consider while buying a hydroponics system that suits your requirements and guarantees you value for money.

1. Space Accessible

First of all, you need to analyze the rising platform to evaluate the room available. This is because the number of pots or buckets that may be used in a given hydroponic system is dictated by the place accessible. Ultimately, that will decide the number of crops you will produce at your mounting location.

The smaller hydroponic systems need about 16 square feet of floor space in most situations. You will also plan an extra room for housing the water tank, indoor rising lighting network, generator, and coolers. Examining the room available for the increasing platform is also a crucial requirement.

2. Automation

Hydroponics systems have additional components such as pumps, growing lamps, and coolers, which are necessary when growing plants to ensure maximum rates are achieved. There are both automated and manual systems on the market, and the gardener must choose the best method which provides performance.

Recent work has found that much loss in indoor planting is attributed to inadequate temperature regulation and water levels. Buying an automated device can give you an easier time as plants are rising because the device can automatically handle the optimal rates needed.

New structures have electronic sensors that control humidity, temperature, lighting, and water levels automatically, thus relieving you of a lot of manual change pressure.

3. Expandability of the Hydroponics System

You will want to start gardening with a small hydroponic device package as a starter, then extend it later to develop more plants. When you are persuaded of the advantages of using this essential and enjoyable form of planting, you should expect to reach the device to accommodate more plants.

In this situation, you need ample room to house additional buckets or pots to handle the extra plants appropriately. Unit expandability defines the total performance, and it's a critical aspect that will help you make the correct decision.

4. Energy efficiency

The growing hydroponic device requires electricity to sustain pumping, lighting, and air conditioning. Especially when a farmer refuses to use energy-LED bulbs, the electricity costs will run high.

Therefore, also ensure that you use energy-LEDs to develop lights while installing your hydroponics device, and that will go a long way to reducing your running expenses.

5. System price and setup costs

Hydroponics systems may be purchased as pre-constructed, or the gardener can decide to install one. Creating your DIY Hydroponics device at home would take professional support, and you'll need to employ a specialist to set up the system if you don't have the resources to do so.

This can be costly for newcomers and needs close monitoring, implying that during deployment, you would have to be present. On the other side, the industry has a wide variety of pre-hydroponics systems that are suited to your choice. With all already in order, you'll just need to configure the machine to your desired position and kick-your indoor gardening venture immediately.

You should make the correct decision based on the spending strategy, whether to purchase DIY or a pre-device.

We hope the above considerations can serve as an eye-opener to help you in making the correct decision while buying a hydroponic system that not only offers you a flourishing soilless gardening experience but also offers you value for money.

List of Fruits and Their Gardening Techniques

Hydroponics is a plant-growing process in water and without soil. At optimal levels, minerals and nutrients are applied to the water such that the plants can commit their resources to grow fruits and vegetables, resulting in higher production.

You can produce just about everything using the hydroponics. In a hydroponic greenhouse here is our top ten fruits & veggies to grow:

Tomatoes

Vining plants such as tomatoes are suitable for indoor gardens because they need a limited amount of ground space so you would have room up to the ceiling to train them. Being able to track and regulate the nutrients obtained by the plant helps the grower to experience a consistent harvest during the year, without losing flavor. Tomatoes are a vitamin A, C, and folic acid-rich plant. We contain potent antioxidants that help protect against the risk of heart disease, diabetes, and cancer.

Lettuce

For hydroponic gardeners, Lettuce is a top option since it needs little room, little attention, and you can harvest leaves as it develops. In a couple of weeks, you'll get your first harvest so you can reap the benefits of your first crispy seed. Lettuce is a very low-calorie veg, which contains phytonutrients that promote health and prevent properties from the disease. Rich in vitamins A, C, and K, it includes minerals such as copper, calcium magnesium, and potassium, essential for body metabolism, etc.

Cumber

Water-loving fruits make your hydroponic garden a good pick. Given ample room and concomitant help, cucumbers should develop abundantly. The cucumbers are high in copper, sodium, potassium, magnesium, calcium, and zinc micro-. They produce vitamins B, C, and folic acid. Such components render cucumbers effective in cleaning up the body from cholesterol, slowing down the aging cycle, and regulating metabolism.

Spring onion

In reality, spring onions are very young onions harvested until the bulb gets swelling and that. One-pot will sprout thousands of onions and harvest every three to four weeks! The antioxidants in spring onions aid by inhibiting the activity of free radicals from avoiding harm to DNA and cellular tissue. Spring onions are filled with vitamins C and K, both essential to healthy bones. Natural properties of spring onions are more widely used for curing respiratory illnesses such as fever and colds. These include vitamins B and A, as well.

Peppers

Peppers can grow under somewhat similar conditions to tomatoes, but increasing nighttime temperatures and declining daytime temperatures rise the quality of fruit once plants achieve their mature height. Not only do peppers bring taste and spice to your diet, but they are small in calories and rich in vitamins and nutrients. Full with vitamins A and C and a steady supply with protein, folic acid, and potassium, giving them valuable properties in the battle against infection and disease.

Spinach

Just like lettuce, other leafy vegetables like spinach grow well in hydroponic systems. When you leave it picked, spinach develops rapidly and is abundant. Spinach is an extremely nutritious green leafy vegetable whose antioxidant effects are well established. It provides calcium, sugar, nutrients, and vitamins. Spinach is a source of vitamins A, C, K, F, magnesium, folic acid, iron, zinc, and many others rendering it one of the healthiest green leafy vegetables to go. It strengthens the skin, decreases cholesterol, improves metabolism, prevents aging, and offers a plentiful iron supply.

Strawberries

In damp environments, strawberries flourish and grow well under hydroponic environments. Providing fruits that are larger than in dirt and will have harvest during the year. Strawberries, which are well known immune boosters, are rich in antioxidants and vitamin c. They also aid in lowering cholesterol and high blood pressure

Blueberries

Blueberries allow healthy acidic conditions in the soil and therefore develop best under hydroponic conditions. It's much easier to control the ph content and nutrients and will allow a much more abundant, safer harvest. Blueberries are widely known to be rich in antioxidants that support the nervous system and the brain. They are ranked among the highest fruits needed to provide antioxidants and vitamins for a safe body.

Basil

Herbs are a popular alternative because little maintenance is needed and can yield a fantastic crop. Not only do herbs have flavor and scent, but they do provide a wide variety of applications for wellness. Research shows that basil helps to reduce inflammation and swelling, is high in antioxidants, and helps protect against free radicals that trigger aging.

Coriander

Coriander is a fantastic growing herb that requires just around 4 weeks and can yield 2-3 harvests. This doesn't need any particular criteria, so you'll get the best crop though plenty of suns. Coriander has numerous advantages for the skin. It includes vitamin c, vitamin k, and calcium, as well as magnesium, iron, and starch. Aid for irritation of the eyes, elevated cholesterol, oral ulcers, vomiting, and many other illnesses is well established.

Tips to Grow the Healthy Plants

The description below of plant growing tips should help you find (and eliminate) issues in your yard.

1. Take the time to build the right environment before there come new plants. The most important thing are going to do with your flowers is useful soil preparation. Lose soil to 6 inches or more, add

organic matter (e.g., peat moss or manure), and mix well. Rake the stage till. Soil preparation can be a fun activity, one that enhances the anticipation of life, much like having the nursery ready for a new child.

2. Do not smother young plants with alot thick a soil cover. Many flower seeds can be covered lightly; make the layer of soil just 1/4 inch thick. To date, planting flower seeds is a ordinary mistake, like new parents, who seem to get too many covers covering an infant. Sowing depth and planting time, critical to the growth of modern life, are situations where expert advice can be provided. Cover the seed packet, then cover it once again.

1. Using fast foods or healthy foods but spurts well nourish young plants during development. Through applying soluble fertilizers to the watering tank, you are feeding fast foods to your fast-growing plants. If these fertilizers, which are filled with toxic chemicals, are not the way you want to feed young people, you can opt to go organic with slower-moving but better compost, fish fertilizer, or manure fertilizer. One correct choice of food is to serve a batch of manure tea home-brewed. Slower-acting organic crops do not seem to suit the short and active lives of your teenage plants, but in the longer term, you will build a better soil environment for upcoming generations of flower.

4. If the plants are young, harmful items are weeded out. The type of mates your flowers stick with will influence how direct and durable as adults in this spot of accelerated growth. Weeds rob the seedlings of water and important nutrients and make them look poor. If a healthy flower garden descends, you can always blame the effect on the bulbs of the weedy companions. Take a stand and remain in control; set limits, and spend time pulling weeds.

5. Be overprotective on the delicate seedling stage of a plant. They will be at the delicate scale of seedling or the infant when seeds have sprouted. It is your role, at this point, to float over them. Hold the soil fertile, but avoid the urge to fertilize until you find some real leaves. The fertilization of freshly sprouted seeds is like trying to feed a young pork chop: it doesn't go down smoothly, so it can be risky. While it is like waiting for a child to get teeth to wait for the first set of real leaves, it is the developmental marker that means it's time for a dietary change.

6. Plants with deadheads to make them look young. Keep the color flowing by deadheading or cutting dying fruit heads after the plants have flowered. You can also seek to revitalize it by shaving off the fading flowers, and one- of the top growth when your flowering plant fades (or starts to look ready for retirement). Donate fertilizer now. This trick restores plant productivity and flowering "past its generation."

7. Provide assistance as plants ripen and grow tall. As seedlings,

encourage any extra support to transform into teenage ganglion plants. Now is the time to have forked twigs or other supports before the plants survive the rainstorms of life. You will also pinch the midpoint of young flowering plants to encourage more bushy side growth, like petunias and fuchsias. Tall sunflower and dahlias can need tied stakes. (These pinching and binding methods for raising babies are not allowed, no matter how much you want to squeeze them and bind them during rapid teenage development.)

8. Adoption of plant is an alternative. Not all extensive flower gardens (like families) have to be produced by planting the seed yourself. Transplantation from a nursery may be a simpler option, or you might want to start the seeds indoors, then transfer them cautiously to the outdoor nursery until the weather has cooled down. The first few nights are important, no matter where the transplants start, as the young plants have to adapt or harden to a new environment. Let them chill outside under a screened porch or patio for a few days. And, if rooted, cover them with a light sheet and newspaper tents to give a safe nighttime blanket. Pondering about is hardening- time as a half- kindergarten, which can help flower children make the transition from home all day.

9. Celebrate as a Perennials member. There will be a time when plants, in particular for perennials, need to adjust. Being too big for their first home is one indicator you've done the best with your parenting. There's no need to feel anxious about this moment of divergence. Some perennials can be quickly divided by cutting side shoots of the mother or baby plants and transporting them to a new site. When you do that on a rainy day, and by loosen the soil and water well prepare the new house, this step will be easier for all.

10. Picture your achievements fully grown and flourishing! Let the camera out and take pretty pictures of your lovely flowers in the middle of their lives. Gather a new bouquet to take indoors, or celebrate the joy of plant rearing by offering a vase of fresh- triumph to your neighbors or relatives.

CHAPTER 9
FREQUENTLY ASKED QUESTIONS

Is hydroponic gardening better than normal gardening?

Everyone has their preferred way of gardening, and as long as you get the expected results, the best of these two is a matter of perspective. In principle, however, hydroponic gardening is better than normal gardening for several reasons. The fact that you can grow more plants in the same space compared to a normal soil garden means that you are looking at the prospect of a higher yield.

In hydroponics gardening, you provide nutrients to the roots of your plants instead of them stretching through the soil in search of nutrition. Hydroponic gardens allow you to stack plants together, improving your chances of success by maximizing space. Since you provide all the nutrients, water, and oxygen your plants need, they have access to more oxygen than a soil garden. This enables your plants to absorb more nutrients and experience a higher growth rate. Besides, it is easier to control the nutrient level your plants consume in a hydroponics garden than a normal soil garden.

Is it possible to grow a hydroponic garden outside?

Yes, you can grow your hydroponic garden outside. However, you must be prepared to deal with managing fluctuating temperatures from time to time. To manage temperature, you have to install heaters and chillers in the hydroponic garden. If you live in an area where power is too expensive, you can build the reservoirs into the ground. This will not only help in regulating the temperature but will also give you a natural approach to hydroponic gardening.

Managing temperature is important because when the temperature is too high, this creates a conducive environment for the growth of anaerobic bacteria that will harm your plants. If the temperature is too cold, it will stunt the growth of your plants.

Is it possible to grow organic plants?

You can grow anything you want in a hydroponic garden as long as you have the right system, sufficient nutrients, and growth conditions. For organic produce, you must be careful about the growth conditions and ensure your hydroponics system is kept clean throughout.

That being said, most of the plants you come across can thrive in a hydroponics farm. However, it is relatively difficult to grow some plants in a specific hydroponic system. This comes down to certain factors, such as the fact that some plants thrive in a wet system while others do not; some plants grow heavier when they start bearing fruits or flowering; other plants just need a little bit of water. However, most plants that are grown from seeds will thrive in a hydroponic garden.

Can I use one hydroponic system to grow a variety of plants?

Indeed. You can grow as many plant varieties as you wish in a hydroponic system. However, you must make sure you know the necessary growth requirements for each plant variety. You will also need an elaborate hydroponic system, such as the drip system to make this work.

It is wise to start with a small farm with similar plants, then start diversifying the crops gradually. For example, you can have flowering vegetables and tomatoes in one system and leafy vegetables in another. Remember that as the plant variety increases, it will be increasingly difficult for you to accommodate all plants.

How do I unclog the pump?

Cleaning your equipment regularly will help. Soak the equipment in hot water and add a tablespoon of bleach for every gallon of water as a cleansing agent. Scrub the pump with a brush to remove any debris; rinse and air the pump out to dry.

What can I do about algae in my hydroponic system?

The best algae management solution is proactive prevention. You simply need to make sure the conditions in the growth room are not favorable for algae growth. With this in mind, keep the reservoir lid closed and the nutrient solution away from light.

If algae are already in the system, you can use a brush or solution of hydrogen peroxide to remove it. If the algae particles are floating in the nutrient solution, flush the growth chamber and reservoir tank with clean water, then start a new nutrient solution.

How do I tell the difference between organic and inorganic fertilizers?

Organic fertilizers come from natural organic compounds, including worm castings, manure, and compost. Inorganic fertilizers are made through chemical processes using inorganic compounds. For your plants, both fertilizers have similar nutrient levels. Most organic fertilizers require symbiotic bacteria and fungi to break them down. You might notice, however, that some organic nutrients result in sludge accumulating in the reservoir tank. If you are using organic nutrients, do not use hydrogen peroxide because it kills all the useful bacteria and fungi.

What do PPM and EC mean?

PPM refers to parts per million. It is a common measurement in hydroponics to determine how much total dissolved solids are present in your nutrients or the amount of carbon dioxide in the atmosphere.

EC refers to the electrical conductivity of the nutrient solution. With an EC meter, an electrical voltage is applied to the nutrient solution, after which you can read the conductivity from the mineral ions.

Is it safe to transfer plants from a soil garden to a hydroponic garden?

Yes, you can transfer plants easily. First, make sure you wash the roots in running water to eliminate as much soil from them as possible. You must also be cautious with the roots because plants can suffer transplant shock if not handled well. After the roots are clean, transplant them in isolation for a while to make sure that the plant is not infected before you move it to your hydroponic garden.

Why do hydroponic plants taste better than soil garden plants?

This often happens because hydroponic plants have access to all the nutrients needed for growth. In a soil garden, the plants might not have this luxury. The roots might have to extend further to the necessary nutrients, and they might still suffer deficiencies depending on the nature of the soil.

How do I determine whether my seeds are viable?

A simple way to do this is to pre-soak them. Fill a glass with distilled water and add the seeds inside, then leave it for 24 hours. The viable seeds will sink to the bottom of the glass. Floating seeds are not viable and will not germinate.

GROWTH LIGHTS

Is it okay to grow plants indoors using natural sunlight?

Yes, this is perfectly fine. You can still benefit from natural sunlight, depending on where you set your plants. You can have the plants beside your windows or in a greenhouse. Apart from that, you can also use solar tubes and skylights to light up your garden. However, you must take care not to interrupt the dark cycle plants go through, especially if you are growing plants that need prolonged periods of darkness uninterrupted.

Are grow lights harmful to my eyes?

As a safety precaution, you should never look directly into grow lights because they have the potential to damage your retina. However, you can still work in an area that is illuminated with HID lighting. If you work for a long period in an area illuminated by HID lighting, you might suffer strained eyesight.

You should have a protective cover for your eyes in light of the UV rays that are emitted by grow lights. Apart from that, you also need to consider correcting the color that is emitted by grow lights to a natural appearance as this will help you identify pests and diseases faster. The earlier you can identify problems, the sooner you can look for solutions.

What are the ideal types of lighting necessary for indoor plant growth?

There are different types of lights that you can use for your indoor garden. Here are some of the options you have:

- LED lights

- Induction lights

- Fluorescent lights

- Sulfur plasma lights

- High-pressure sodium lights (HPS)

- Metal halide lights

Whichever of these lights you choose, remember to check the plant requirements to ensure you choose the appropriate lights for your garden.

Do I need high-pressure sodium lighting?

First, a high-pressure sodium light produces light by discharging sodium through a gas discharge process. HPS lights have been in use for years for indoor gardening because of their ability to produce light between the orange and red spectrum, which is ideal for many indoor plants. This spectrum is important because it is within that range that flowering plants can produce flowers. In the case of flowers and fruit-bearing plants, HPS has proven effective in delivering high yields over the years.

Before you decide to use HPS lights, however, you must consider the flip side. While they are responsible for high yields, these lights are ineffective in terms of the amount of heat that they generate. By design, most of the light produced by HPS lights comes from under the lamp. This makes it difficult to disperse light evenly. As a result, you have a better chance of success with fewer large indoor plants than smaller plants.

The problem of light dispersion can, however, be tackled by using LED and induction lamps. These two types of lights are more efficient in the even dispersion of light. Other than that, they also reduce your average spending on air cooling or ventilation systems.

Do I need fluorescent lighting?

Fluorescent lights use low-pressure mercury vapor to produce light. Fluorescent lights are more efficient compared to normal incandescent lights. For indoor plants, the most common fluorescent lights are compact fluorescents and the T5 fluorescent. If you have a large indoor garden, T5 fluorescent lights are ideal because they can spread light evenly over a large area. This makes it a good option for cuttings or seedlings.

Compact fluorescent lights, on the other hand, are ideal for smaller areas because of their intensity. They are, therefore, ideal for larger indoor plants, especially if you are only growing a few plants. Generally, fluorescent lights are ideal not just for plant cuttings and seedlings but also for any indoor plants that require low light.

Do I need induction lamps?

The best way to answer this question is to understand how induction lights work. First, this type of light does not have electrodes. Therefore, they produce lights through an electromagnetic field. Electrodes usually reduce the lifespan of lamps, so without them, induction lamps last longer than most lamps. They also produce the same output of light as a normal fluorescent lamp. However, they are better than fluorescent lights because the produced light is better optimized for indoor plant growth. Induction lamps are ideal if you are growing a lot of short plants. In fact, most growers are increasingly starting to use them in modern greenhouses because of their longevity and efficiency.

What is the use of a reflector?

One of the common challenges you experience when growing plants indoors is that some plants might not receive all the light necessary for growth. This is where a reflector comes in. The role of a reflector is to disperse light toward all plants. From the focal point, lamps produce light at 360 degrees. With a reflector, you can redirect the light that goes upwards back to the plant canopy, so the light is not wasted.

How long should grow lights stay on?

Each grower has their preferred lighting duration. For most vegetative plants, 18 hours is sufficient, with 6 hours of complete darkness. However, some growers leave their lights on for 24 hours. The 18:6 schedule is ideal because it resembles a normal daylight system. Besides, your plants enjoy exponential growth while, at the same time, saving you on energy consumption.

The ideal lighting system also depends on the kind of plants you are growing. When the daylight duration is reduced, Some plants flower. In this case, you can reduce your lighting system from 18:6 to 12:12. Take note that the 18:6 system is ideal for plants that generally flower when they mature and will use this system for most of their lives.

What is the ideal distance between my plants and the grow light?

The recommended distance depends on different factors. If you are using induction lamps and fluorescent lamps, the perfect distance should be around 6 inches from the tops of your plants. These lights generate low heat.

If you are using LED grow lights, the best distance should be between 9 and 12 inches. For HID lights, it depends on the individual wattage. If you are using 400W, the ideal distance is between 12 and 16 inches, 16 to 20 inches for 600W, and 18 to 24 inches for 1000W.

If you are using an air-cooled reflector alongside your grow light, you can reduce the distance between the plants and the lamp. Generally, the rule of thumb is to measure the ideal distance using your hand. If the temperature is comfortable for your hand, it is probably comfortable for your plants too.

Is it okay to change bulbs from one hydroponic system to another?

Bulbs used in hydroponics are made specifically for the system they operate in. Therefore, you should never interchange them. For example, a 400-watt bulb should not be used in a 250-watt hydroponic system. Using the wrong bulb increases the risk of instability, and the bulb might explode.

On the same note, do not use HPS bulbs in a halide bulb system. The ballast in each system is built specifically to run the type of bulb it is rated for. Remember that the ratings are assigned after careful analysis and testing. Even if you are using conversion bulbs, make sure you install them in the correct system.

WATER & NUTRITION

Should I adjust the nutrient solution pH?

Yes, you should. The difference between a hydroponic garden and a soil garden is that soil can create a safe buffer for pH imbalance. If the pH is not perfect for the plant, the soil makeup can balance the pH to a reasonable level for the plants. Without soil, therefore, it is up to you to balance the pH accordingly. The correct nutrient level makes it easier for plants to absorb as many nutrients as possible for healthy growth.

Is it a must that I use water from reverse osmosis or distilled water?

While these types of water are quite efficient, it is not mandatory. A good portion of plant nutrients include minerals that already exist in water. Most water will work just fine. However, if you need complete control over the nutrient levels in your hydroponic garden, distilled and reverse osmosis water might be the best option.

When using purified water, make sure you replenish the magnesium and calcium levels to have a good nutrient solution. One problem you will have with purified water is that the lack of minerals makes it difficult to create a pH buffer for your plants. Therefore, you might have a difficult time stabilizing the water pH, but by adding magnesium and Calcium, this problem should be sorted out.

Is there a recommended pH level for hydroponic gardens?

All requirements for your hydroponic garden will depend on the unique plant needs. However, most plants generally thrive in a pH range between 5.5 and 6.2

Can I use well water for my hydroponic garden?

This is not an easy question to answer without analyzing the water sample. In most cases, well water is hard water; therefore, you must use it alongside nutrients specially made for hard water. Alternatively, you can purify the water through reverse osmosis to eliminate the excess minerals.

Why is the pH in my garden fluctuating?

When you monitor the pH in your garden, you will notice that one or two days later, it might have jumped, perhaps from 5.5 to 6.0. Is this okay? Yes, it is okay. Remember that most nutrients you add to the setup are acidic. Once the plants absorb them, it is normal for the neutral pH to rise, as the environment around the roots becomes acidic too. Therefore, pH upheavals in the reservoir tank should not concern you too much. It is normal. When the pH drops, this is an indication that your solution has a lot of nutrients. Besides, plants absorb nutrients better at different pH levels. This fluctuation allows them to absorb all the nutrients they need for healthy growth.

CONCLUSION

Everybody enjoys hobbies throughout their leisure time. Some people might have more than one hobby. Well, here's one among us for those gardeners and arborists. Consider hydroponic gardening indoors as an entertaining hobby. You will enjoy indoor hydroponic gardening if you love gardens and make things grow. Hydroponic gardening is the same as regular planting unless there is no mess at all. Indoor hydroponic gardening has no soil. Have you ever seen the famous Babylon Hanging Gardens? This is one of the world's Seven Wonders and is probably the earliest evidence of our indoor hydroponic gardening in human history.

Very few people now have the resources to produce something as luxuriant as this earthly wonder, but in a hydroponic greenhouse, we can grow our minibar. It is the same as a regular greenhouse, but hydroponic because all plants are grown with water, light, and air.

That is false. That is right. There is no need for soil, and this is exactly what indoor hydroponic gardening is about. When growing in a hydroponic greenhouse, your favorite fruits and vegetables is the latest fad among gardeners. Everything you need is here, and if you want to go to the local pond and garden shop and hydroponic packages. Or you test all the wonderful might make your own.

Recommendation to a novice, however, is to get one of the hydroponic kits. Many people use one of the two popular hydroponic kits: a hydroponic ebb and flow kit or a hydroponic deep culture

Pack. These would be simple and basic hydroponic packages all your hydroponic greenhouse needs to start. If you want to extend your hydroponic greenhouse, you will probably have to buy additional lights and more nutrient solutions. Nonetheless, it's a good investment in the long run.

Scientific studies show that hydroponic greenhouse goods are lighter, juicier, and more nutritious than store purchases. The additional bonus is that there are almost no weed issues that outdoor gardens usually face. In a hydroponic greenhouse, there are very few pests. This, in turn, means that harmful and dangerous pesticides and insecticides are not needed. Another great advantage is that you can cultivate your favorite fruit and vegetables throughout the year with hydroponic kits. Yeah! Wow! How cool this is! You could at whatever time of the year grow your food, protect your family from harmful chemicals, and enjoy your favorite foods.

Hydroponic indoor gardening is a wonderful hobby. There is practically no clutter, no additives, and many benefits can be seen in the eye. You grow a garden that you enjoy and avoid all the downsides and headaches that usually come with gardening. Go out, then, if you want to try something new. Take some of your mates, go to the store and purchase hydroponic kits and make your hydroponic greenhouse. Then sit back and enjoy your favorite food whenever you want.

Hydroponics is the science of soilless plant growth by using minerals dissolved in water. You will discover in this guide all the resources, techniques, and strategies for creating a viable, soil-free hydroponic garden filled with vibrant and healthy plants.

Hydroponics developed from Latin geoponics, meaning agricultural work and hydro, meaning water is the science of plants growing instead of soil using a solution of appropriate nutrients. Hydroponics can be used to develop many plant forms successfully.

The plants are grown in soil in traditional gardening and receive their nutrients from the chemical compounds in the soil. Hydroponic gardener replaces soil with a balanced, nutrient-rich solution that is easily absorbable by the plant. It saves energy, which can be used for more robust growth, as the plant does not work hard to absorb the nutrients available.

Because of this energy-saving, plants cultivated with these hydroponic methods outperform plants developed both in growth and fruit production.

Due to reliable performance and good profit margins, growing numbers of commercial growers are turning to hydroponic growth. With specially formulated organic nutrients, complete organic production is possible, providing healthy, cheap vegetables, and herbs.

There are many different forms of the hydroponic system, but they all obey the same basic concept of plants providing nutrients and water. The most common methods are aquaculture, nutrition, and aquaculture.

This is a hydroponic system in which plant roots are immersed with a complex combination of dissolved nutrients in the water.

As you can see, when setting up a hydroponic system, there are some things you need to keep an eye on or remember. You'll cover nearly all with the basics of your water and nutrients, the lighting effect, and ventilation.

Any of this depends on your growing room, and whether you have access to external windows or it is sealed off, and you rely on rising lights to the maximum. If you are in charge of these basic principles, you are in a position to take on any hydroponic system, since the same basic rules are the same.

Once you know the basics, you can extend any program easily, or create a larger one from scratch. The exploration of new ideas and methods is a lot of fun, but these basics will never change. Nonetheless, you know your experiences, and whatever information you want to use, we hope you can find the knowledge.

CPSIA information can be obtained
at www.ICGtesting.com
Printed in the USA
BVHW040213050421
604204BV00017B/1208